HEAL, MY SON!

HEAL, MY SON!

The Amazing Story of John Cain

by

PETER GREEN

PART II

by

JOHN CAIN

Published for
JOHN CAIN
by Van Duren Publishers

© Copyright 1977 and 1985: John Cain

First edition published in September 1977
by Van Duren Contract Publications Limited,
Gerrards Cross, Buckinghamshire.

Second enlarged edition published September 1985 for John Cain by
Van Duren Publishers, Gerrards Cross, Buckinghamshire.

ISBN Second Edition 0-905715-27-6

Produced in Great Britain
Set by Grove Graphics, Tring, Hertfordshire
Printed by Billing & Sons Limited, Worcester

PREFACE
by
Bryce Bond

WHEN asked to write this preface, I was greatly pleased and flattered to be associated with John Cain, the subject, and the writer, Peter Green. Equally I am proud to be a practising National Federation of Spiritual Healers' member.

For many years I have investigated and researched the area of parapsychology and its related realms. I have been an active healer for over 15 years. I was able to express my profound feelings for this humbling work through magazines and television. Writing for psychic journals is indeed exciting; but propagating truth is a dedication.

I have interviewed hundreds of healers, mediums, psychics and members of the orthodox medical profession. I have watched the great healers at work, including John Cain. He and the other dedicated ones truly reflect God's light. For this energy, power and love all come from the God-head. Here in this vast United States we have many healers separated by huge distances. In Great Britain, by contrast, they are closer.

Healing is a cherished gift. We healers gladly, and humbly, dedicate our lives to an inspiring cause which we *know* is right. They demonstrate compassion and empathy, a loving desire to help the afflicted. The reward is in seeing a patient respond to spirit healing and become whole again after the doctors gave up.

Most healers accept that they act as a channel, just like a human radio receiver, for people in the spirit world. These disembodied souls, often doctors when on earth, actually accomplish the diagnosing and healing. Disease is caused by an imbalance of the life energy flowing through the body. Mesmer and his flock claimed to heal with 'magnetic' energy. Some psychic healers say they work on a person's 'etheric' energy. But most healers I know function through a higher intelligence called God!

We shall see that this palpable failure of physicians to view the patient as a whole, rather than as the sum of his or her symptoms, has, as much as any other single factor, been propelling more and more discouraged sufferers into the realm of unorthodox healing. Today, as hundreds of John Cain's patients will happily testify, people in ever increasing number are turning to alternative forms of the healing arts. Conventional doctors are being forced to recognise that people are being restored to health by methods far removed from what passes as standard medical practice in the United States and Great Britain.

Millions suffer from severe and chronic disorders, many deemed incurable by orthodox practitioners. But many, in a stubborn quest for relief from their miseries, have been helped and sometimes cured by these strangely unorthodox methods. Unlike orthodox allopathy, when doctors treat only the symptoms, spirit healing triumphs because it works on the cause. You might call it a spiritual exercise from the Other Side. A fusion of spirits, including the patient's naturally, results in removing disharmony between spirit, mind and body. This is the essence, the secret, of spirit healing. And this is what orthodox medicine in its well-preserved ignorance, fails to grasp.

Most healers are passive channels with total trust in God, as with John Cain. When personal ego is extinguished, and Cain makes way for God, 'miracles' happen. Cain thanks God for allowing him to do His work.

I was attracted more and more to the reports of Cain's work and his growing list of impressive successes. I knew I had to see and talk to this man from Liverpool.

In November, 1976, my chance came. With a very good friend and author, Rebecca Hall, I took a morning train to Merseyside, which was packed with soccer fans – and more than a dash of mayhem! Amid the exciting madness at Liverpool's grimy Lime Street station, we hailed a taxi to take us to Cain's healing sanctuary.

The sun penetrated the dark clouds as we arrived at his bungalow. Two huge Labradors barked a noisy welcome. Cain greeted us at the door. I felt I had known this man all my life. His warmth and honesty were apparent. What warmed me to him was his total dedication to the work of healing God's flock. He knows the more he frees the ego the stronger the healing.

I admired his statement that every healer should be tested and graded. It was no surprise to find he was expecting Angus McHutchon, a scientist and Society of Psychical Research member. Apart from McHutchon, Cain has been scientifically tested by Dr John Taylor, professor of applied mathematics at London's King's College. His results were not available for this publication.

I was impressed to learn that McHutchon's records show that a fantastic 95 per cent of patients respond to John Cain's treatment. His many miraculous healings include a hole-in-the-heart baby and a brain cancer sufferer given only three months to live. Many patients are convinced they have been permanently cured by Cain and his spirit world team who came to the rescue after traditional medicine failed.

Cain is a phenomenon. Scientific examination has shown that his brain wave sequences register a very high-alpha state. He seems to transfer this brain condition to patients. They lapse into trance when the healing process begins. In a comatose state they find their limbs being manipulated and bodies raised without the healer touching them.

We were invited to observe Cain at work in his sanctuary. Armed with tape recorders and a camera, and McHutchon with his array of electronic equipment, we watched an attractive young woman sit on a stool in the centre of the room. Cain was hooked to a galvanic skin response meter which measures changes in electrical resistance. Within seconds of placing his hands over the woman's head, she went into light trance. The galvanometer needle showed that Cain was in a high-alpha state of mind, yet fully conscious.

This was exciting. Next we watched the patient being manipulated by some force. Rapidly her arms went up and down. Her legs swished rhythmically. She seemed to be more flexible in her movements than a Yoga instructor.

Refreshingly Cain is always willing to experiment to increase and vary the beneficial spirit world power. Most patients get a copy of his photograph. Remarkable reports have emanated that people experience a trance state merely by looking at it and then feel healing manipulation within their bodies. Unseen 'hands' work wasted muscles. Many 'photo patients' report incredible results.

What I saw next in his sanctuary still amazes me to this day. An elderly woman was treated. Earlier she almost had to be carried into the bungalow. Crippled with acute arthritis for many years, she had also suffered heart attacks. I could hardly believe what happened. But it did. The sensor monitoring her brain wave patterns moved into the high-alpha state. She was completely 'out'. Then the unseen energy began its work. Her arms and legs moved very fast. She was being lifted up and down from the couch. You knew she didn't have the strength to do it. The energy was so powerful we felt enveloped.

I have experienced many exciting scenes in my life. But this was ultra-beautiful. I felt tremendous love filling the room. The old woman came to, smiled and stretched easily, saying she felt as though reborn.

I was his next patient. I sensed a higher intelligence guiding the whole operation. It felt marvellous. Cain placed his hands over the solar plexus. I felt a sensation of electrical energy. It was tremendously, invigoratingly soothing. I just wanted to remain in this hugely blissful state. The most beautiful colours filled my mind as Cain passed a hand over my head. If I had to imagine the presence of God, this would be it.

In conclusion, I can say only that John Cain is the most remarkable healer I have ever met. He is truly guided and inspired. I know that he will be one of the world's greatest healers! As you read the graphic ensuing account, I believe you will appreciate the reasons for my statement.

New York
June 1977

INTRODUCTION

BEING assistant editor to 'Psychic News', the independent Spiritualist weekly, provided an unparalleled, if not unique, opportunity to familiarise myself with the supernormal. For over 30 years' before my association with 'Psychic News' my journalistic experience ranged far and wide, from Fleet Street to suburbia. I was trained to observe and record events.

Dealing with the public and officialdom at all levels, I believe most reporters adopt a professionally sceptical outlook. Invariably one is much concerned with people's fraudulent aspect, in Spiritualism as in general affairs. Nothing can be taken at its face value. Thus cynicism and incredulity have a vital place in the reporter's mental approach to people who may claim outstanding powers.

In my case I found it surprisingly easy, despite my practical training, to accept the reality of spirit healing. The simple key to understanding the phenomena is to recognise that these are natural laws in operation. Scientists, with notably few exceptions, continue to fence-sit, attempting to offer so-called rational explanations for the phenomenon. They continue to disregard the increasing number of men, women, children and animals who recover from a multitude of illnesses, including cancer, due to natural healing, often accomplished after being written-off by the medical profession.

My experience shows that people investigate the subject and become irresistibly convinced of the efficacy of spirit healing. People capable of reasonable judgments usually cannot deny the startling evidence of their own eyes. When you see a woman crippled with osteoarthritis walk freely for the first time in 30 years, or a young girl completely recover from a distressing skin allergy which has defied the best medical brains, you *know* inwardly, even if you cannot bring yourself to admit it outwardly, that a vastly superior intelligence is functioning, one that must be discarnate.

One story to impress me greatly during my formative assessment of Spiritualism and its related phenomena concerned the remarkable child healer, Linda Martel of Guernsey in the Channel Isles.

I investigated some of the amazing cures attributed to this tragic, cruelly-crippled girl, whose touch was reputed to be 'magical'. She passed on – Spiritualists never use the term 'died' – aged five on October 20, 1961. Her funeral was attended by 1,000 Guernsey folk whose collective hearts had been touched by the most incredible child healer the world had seen.

But, even more incredibly, Linda's fabled healing power lives on. Apparently hundreds of people have been helped by visiting the little tot's grave at St Sampson's Churchyard, St Peter Port, Guernsey. Many cures, however, have been claimed – and still are – by people all over the country and in different parts of the world, through square-inch pieces of clothing she wore during her short span of earth life.

I can add my personal tribute to the scores received by Linda's devoted father, Roy, who uses her clothing to end pain and suffering. I have a priceless snip of Linda's topcoat which I have employed to amazing effect for the past six years.

As I made contact with other healers, I began to appreciate just what these often maligned servants of God mean to the vast masses of the world's suffering, those virtually cast aside because they cannot respond to orthodox medicine. Without spirit healers to whom could these flotsam and jetsam of medical science turn? They are condemned as 'hopeless, medically-incurable cases'. To have to live without hope, chained to an inevitable fate, must be the ultimate in suffering. The depth of despair cannot be measured.

This is why healers, such as the remarkable John Cain, the subject of my book, are not only the salt of the earth but are among the world's most warm-hearted, compassionate people, convinced that they are undeniably doing God's work. Can it be really doubted that they continue the natural healing administered so freely by Jesus, the greatest healer and psychic of all, 2,000 years ago?

Happily I dedicate this book to spirit healers everywhere. They are the ones entrusted with the inspiring challenge of doing the medically impossible day after day. I am not embarking on a scientific exercise. Spiritualism's literature includes many such accounts by far more illustrious writers than I.

I certainly could not hope to embellish them. I am perfectly content to show through the overwhelming, enlightening experiences of people who *know* they have been saved, that spirit healing triumphs against the odds. Is it really necessary to know more?

CHAPTER I

NEW STAR IS BORN

THE smart, modern bungalow at 5 Rothesay Drive, Eastham, Wirral, Merseyside, is outwardly no different to the others in the road. But a stranger trying to fathom why it should be the most eagerly sought address in this preponderantly middle-class area would soon arrive at the common denominator. For nearly all the people calling there are in trouble. The majority are medical write-offs. Orthodox medicine has decreed: 'You are on your own, brothers and sisters. We have exhausted our supplies of pill and drug. There is nothing more we can do to help you. You must learn to live (or die?) with whatever plagues you.'

The human spirit, however, invariably displays a subconscious will to survive. There is something too depressingly, automatically final about a medical death sentence. After the initial shock waves have subsided, often the 'victim' will sit down quietly to appraise his or her position. A calming influence descends. The little voice inside, which we subjugate so ruthlessly when material life is sweet and fulsome, suddenly, in the hour of critical need, wins a long overdue audience with the physical body it inhabits. It whispers advice and comfort to its stricken shell. One is surprised to find oneself thinking in terms of the spiritual. 'If medicos cannot help, who can?' a sufferer may intone. In desperation the mind works frantically, seeking the 'impossible'. One picks up a newspaper or magazine agitatedly searching for – what? With unexpected drama, the heart seems to miss a vital beat as the eye conjures with the words, 'spirit healer'. An account of a discarnate treatment, with a sufferer's ecstatic announcement that he has been cured against all odds, becomes compulsive reading.

Or, simply, a friend, neighbour or stranger may, in a moment of compassion, urge, 'Why not experiment with spiritual healing?' There are many paths to the thousands of practitioners who use only their hands, hearts and minds to achieve what medical science has decreed is 'impossible'.

So it is that the flotsam and jetsam stream in progressively increasing droves to the door of John Cain, 46, a former blacksmith who is convinced he was born to heal. Still a comparatively new star in spirit healing's lustrous firmament, he is now widely reckoned to have taken over the mantle of the great, late Harry Edwards. With a major differentiation ... for even Edwards, who physically manipulated sufferers' bones and joints in achieving his countless cures, could not match Cain's stupefying ability to manipulate limbs, and induce the trance state, *without* touching people.

Famed Glasgow medium Albert Best, one of the most experienced and respected clairvoyants in the Spiritualist ranks, believes Cain is destined for world-wide greatness. 'It is really remarkable,' he says, 'to see those suffering from arthritis, etc., fall asleep, many of them for an hour. The most incredible phenomenon then takes place. Unseen hands work the affected muscles. It has to be seen to be believed.'

Best calls Cain one of the most genuine healers he has seen. 'I have witnessed all kinds of psychic phenomena, but Cain's is the most wonderful. I am not easily fooled.'

The unusual healing technique of allowing his guides to put patients in a comatose state, which is done without suggestion or hypnotism, has created great interest.

Cain's intriguing story is the reverse one; of from riches to rags! Only six years ago he had a successful general smithy business in Wallasey, Cheshire. The opulent signs of success for this short, but powerfully-built man, were there for all to see. In his driveway stood a shining Rolls Royce overshadowing his second choice, a superb Bentley. He had every reason to expect to provide wife Audrey and children John, Jnr, and Jeanette, with life's material luxuries. But something was inexorably nagging Cain, driving a wedge between his loyalties. Most men would opt easily for business success and its related comforts. But Cain knew he was different.

At the age of six he would stroke his mother's temple to banish her frequent migraine attacks. He brought home injured birds for her to tend.

Compassion for living things was a quality that rested easily with John Cain, man and boy.

Years later he was to face an agonising decision, one that only a very special person would be expected to make: Give up the rich life and serve humanity. Reflecting on his boyhood, he recalls an eerie incident that today he regards as having been highly symbolic. He was petrified to 'see' an African lion walking up a path near his home. The young Cain, then only five, ran screaming for sanctuary in adjacent woods. The animal turned out to be a lamb gambolling in the spring sunshine. But to Cain it was the king of the jungle. And the vivid memory remains with him. He certainly had to be lion-hearted in times to come....

At 14 Cain became interested in boxing. He found he had a natural flair for massage. He was in great demand for towelling down the club's young pugilists. They quickly discovered to their delight that any pains wracking their flailed bodies after bouts vanished when Cain's powerful hands massaged them.

Ten days after his 21st birthday in 1950 he joined the Royal Ordnance Corps as a PT instructor. The unit's leave clerk, Jock Gray, who played football for Colchester United, was troubled with a frozen shoulder. Knowing Cain was earning a reputation for massage and manipulation, he asked him to help his sling-held arm. Gray had been having heat treatment at the base hospital. Cain invited him to the gymnasium where he worked on the immobile arm for half-an-hour. Gray, his face wreathed in smiles, rose, flung his arm in the air and threw his sling away. Cain, spirit healer, was in business.

The crucial moment of decision was drawing nearer. But then Cain, however, was enjoying ordinary life too much to be concerned with momentous issues of the future. The spin-off from his first healing was far more pleasurable. To show his appreciation for being restored to soccer fitness, Gray returned to the gymnasium a week later to award Cain a seven-day leave pass with a free travel voucher.

Cain left the Army in 1952, returning to his trade as a blacksmith at Cammell Laird shipbuilders, Birkenhead. After only 12 months the impetuous Cain walked out following a flaming row with his boss. He set his hand to many tasks, including window cleaning, logging and demolition. Then he started his own general smithy business in Wallasey, an old established firm which was practically crumbling to the ground. Over the next four years Cain erected a brand new building and replaced obsolete equipment. A thriving career had begun. He had more money than at any time in his life. The Rolls and Bentley became hallmarks of his success. But, by 1971, Cain found himself wrestling more and more with an inner conflict, a dilemma that only he could solve. The desire to earn money in pursuit of a stable, ultra-comfortable, but somewhat meaningless pattern of life, suddenly had him at war with himself. Another kind of desire was forcing itself to the surface... he knew he was born to heal.

He started leaving the business to run itself as he found his healing hands creating greater demand. He hardly went near it, leaving it to his brother, Mike. As Cain did his healing rounds the business began to slide. He lost interest in it... and thousands of pounds beside.

After a dramatic meeting with his angry bank manager, Cain went to bed a deeply worried man. The inner conflict tearing him from the material path was coming to a head. The big decision, which he had to make for himself and his family, was close at hand.

He tossed about restlessly, finally waking at 3 a.m. He put his head in his hands and sobbed uncontrollably. The conflict was near breaking point. He rose that morning at seven o'clock, and, for no apparent reason, felt his anxieties dissipate. A 'wonderful feeling' enveloped him. He was surrounded inexplicably by an aura of peace and love, as though his pressing material worries did not exist. The ecstatic sensation stayed about half-an-hour. Then, 'clear as a bell,' he psychically heard his 'dead' father say, 'Do not worry; born to heal, Dad.' It was the clincher for Cain. He had been attending numerous Spiritualist churches in Merseyside and elsewhere for several months. Mediums kept pinpointing him, saying, 'You are a healer.'

Now he was convinced his father had returned from the Other Side to urge him to take up his true vocation.

Cain joined a Spiritualist developing circle at Rock Ferry, Birkenhead. There were seven established sitters, one a member for 22 years. During the four weeks he was in the circle, Cain obtained considerable clairvoyance. His powers were functioning with remarkable rapidity. One night, the woman member who had been in the circle for 22 years, proclaimed she had had Long John Silver with her all night. Her companion said: 'Isn't that funny? I've had his parrot perched on my shoulder!'

Forthright Cain exploded with wrath. Sarcastically he asked if the 'communicator' told where he had buried his treasure, adding, 'The best thing we can do is to go back into the silence, find out where he has buried his treasure and then all take a good holiday in the Bahamas.'

The episode finished Cain with Spiritualist circles till he started his own physical one later. Thereafter he was content to develop his psychic powers through his increasingly regular healing activity.

Just before he finally cut all links with his successful business career, he was told about a brain-damaged boy. An inner motivation drove him to locate the child in the hope that he could offer healing. He discovered the boy's address and that the family were Roman Catholics. Though shaking at the prospect of approaching strangers, he summoned up his courage and told the parents he felt he could help their son. He was invited to try and went every morning from ten o'clock to noon. Within three months the treatment had reduced the boy's grotesquely large head by nine inches. The dramatic change startled specialists tending the boy. The story did not have a happy ending because Cain found himself the centre of a family disagreement over whether such unorthodox healing should be allowed to continue. Reluctantly he was forced to withdraw.

His next patient was his daughter, Jeanette, then 13. She was acutely embarrassed by unsightly warts on hands and legs. He laid on his hands. A week later Jeanette was carefree and confident again. The warts had vanished.

This success finally swept from his mind any lingering doubts about what he should do with his remarkable gift. He called a family conference to announce that he was turning over his smithy business to his brother. He had decided, after much torturous thought, to devote his life to full-time healing. Possibly it meant the ultimate in family sacrifice. Overnight, from the day in 1972 he began healing the forsaken sick, the household budget plummeted from a chief executive's rosy salary to zero. Whatever her innermost feelings, Audrey Cain did not turn a hair. Cain assured the family their immediate needs would be provided by the spirit world. Try telling that to the bank manager!

But, despite the first harrowing months when their faith was tested to the utmost, this is exactly what happened. They were, indeed, being looked after by a superior intelligence not of this earth.

CHAPTER 2

FORGES LINK BETWEEN TWO WORLDS

THE forge of his old smithy shop was quickly a forgotten episode as Cain, at first a trifle nervous, but nevertheless displaying great calmness and confidence, opened his door to the outside world. He was about God's business and that meant helping all in need. His and Audrey's home became a thoroughfare. A mere trickle of desperate humanity at first, then a veritable flood, they tramped into the spacious living room to await their turn for treatment in Cain's bare sanctuary, singularly devoid of all religious paraphernalia.

The first 30 people he treated, sporting a variety of complaints, responded encouragingly. Cain, still battling to overcome deep-seated fears, disconcertingly found himself putting each improved case down to coincidence. Could this really be happening? Indeed it could. More and more sufferers announced they had discovered a new zest and sense of purpose in life after being touched by Cain's healing power. Slowly, but surely, his fame began to spread as patients testified to the efficacy of his healing.

Reports began emanating about the wonder of unseen hands manipulating misshapen limbs and wasted muscles during treatment. Cain, it was asserted, did not use his hands. An independent force took over the healing activity so that Cain, the seemingly central figure in the ministrations, was reduced to the role of observer. People being treated were also getting from the medium the added bonus of clairvoyance. Cain's explanation of these supernormal happenings was simple. He believes healing functions through the subconscious mind. 'It's a fusion of minds: mine, the patient's and that of a higher intelligence. That is more than enough for me to know. I am really no wiser today than when I first started laying on hands for the benefit of others. The results speak for themselves. In the earlier stages I could feel my hands being directed to a patient's trouble spots. It is rather like being a blacksmith again, only this time I am convinced that a supernormal

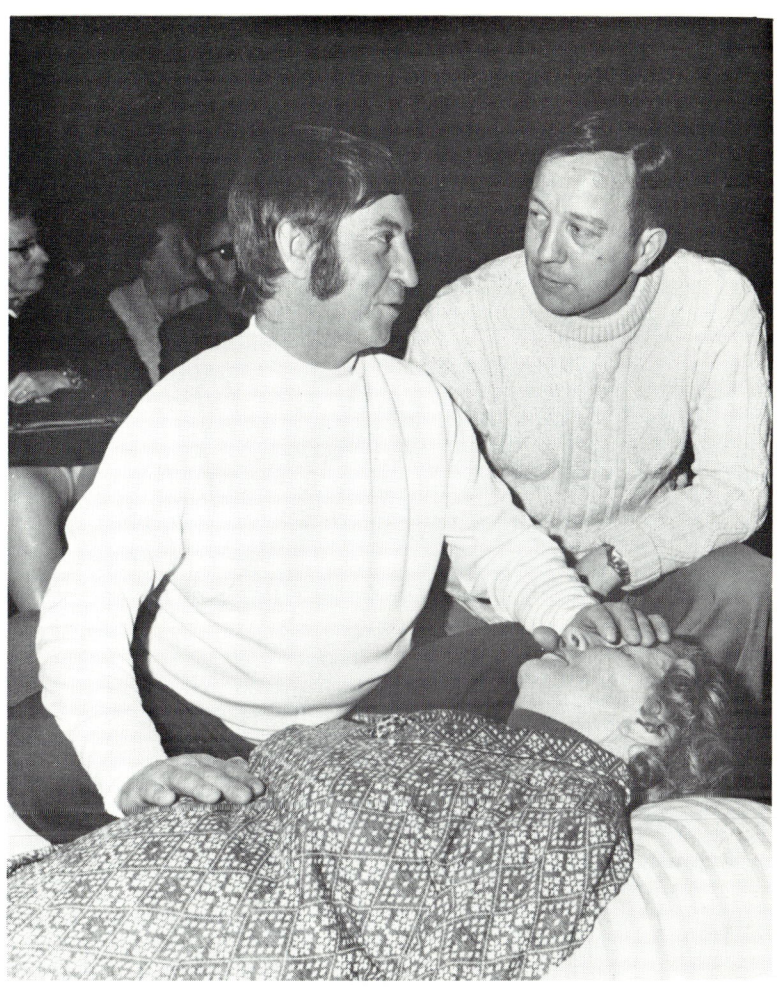

Author Peter Green watches Cain treat a woman at a public healing demonstration at Bromborough Cure Centre in March 1977.

John Cain in one of his earliest healing moments with Karen Guy, then aged three, whose severely dislocated hip was successfully corrected in one treatment.

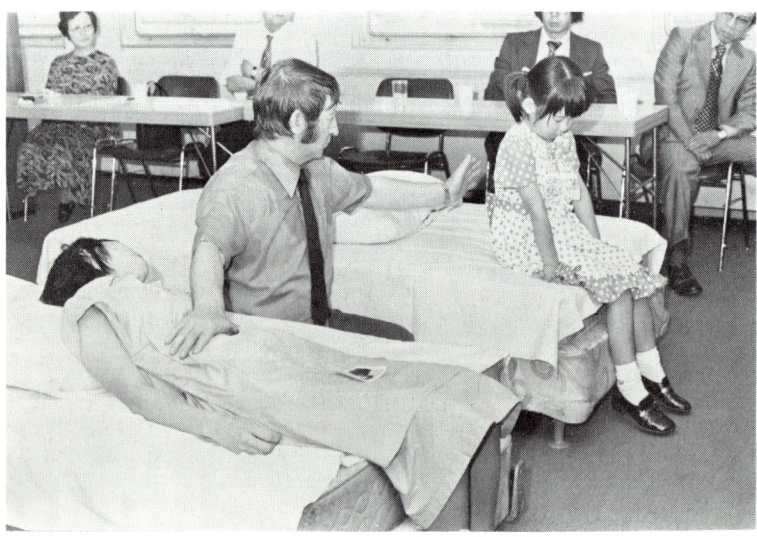

Here Cain displays his ability to treat two young girls at the same time.

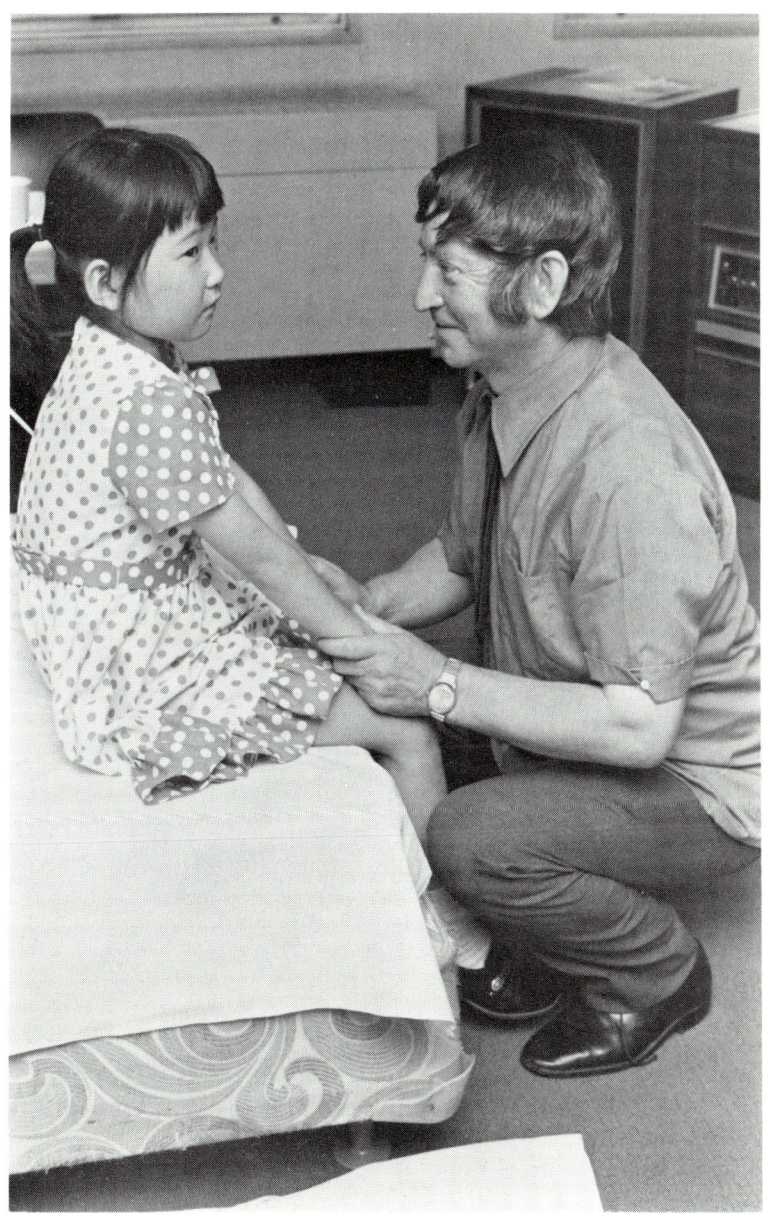

An eight-year-old Tokyo diabetic receives an encouraging smile from the ex-blacksmith as the treatment begins.

link is being forged beween the two worlds. I still work with my hands, but the anvil is no longer a necessary part of my equipment. In fact, the beauty of spirit healing is that there are no cumbrous mechanics involved. The 'equipment' consists entirely of mental vibrations.'

The controlling guide is Dr Carl Heindrich Hoffman who lived his earth life in Austria. Two mediums identified him. The first was trance medium Alan Crossley. Another corroborated the guide's name. It was more than enough for Cain to accept that a 'dead' Austrian doctor works through him. Twice in a week 16 people witnessed Cain's complete disappearance from his sanctuary and Carl, as the guide is affectionately known to all and sundry, materialise in his place. Cain knew he was still there. But he felt that he had been somehow raised above the patients he was treating.

When allowing himself to be used as the healing vessel, Cain's hands alternate between hot and cold. Sometimes he experiences mild electric shocks when working within the aura. He feels the ray leave his hands and penetrate the patient. He experiences a faint vibration in his left hand.

Cain heals seven days a week, often from early morning till late at night. He has become virtually housebound, such is his dedication to the ceaseless job of healing the sick and alleviating pain-wracked bodies. The energies extracted from his body, so that the healing process may operate, leaves him exhausted at the day's end. But he has learned how to pace himself and quickly recovers his vitality so that he is fully charged to begin a new day's work.

He concentrates on each patient for half-an-hour. When asked what keeps him going, and how he can be satisfied to be used as a passive instrument day in and day out, he replies laconically, 'Basically healing is my whole life.' He wants, nor expects, anything more. His ambition is to be the world's finest healer. Many of his patients already regard him as just this. He is certain he has not reached the zenith of his spiritual powers.

Cain believes Carl and the other guides forming his spirit world team are still experimenting with his patients, which accounts for the variety of phenomena in his healings. The manifestations commenced in 1973, nearly a year after Cain had begun his full-time activity. Seated on a stool he was treating a young woman only ten days out of hospital after a hysterectomy. He placed one hand on

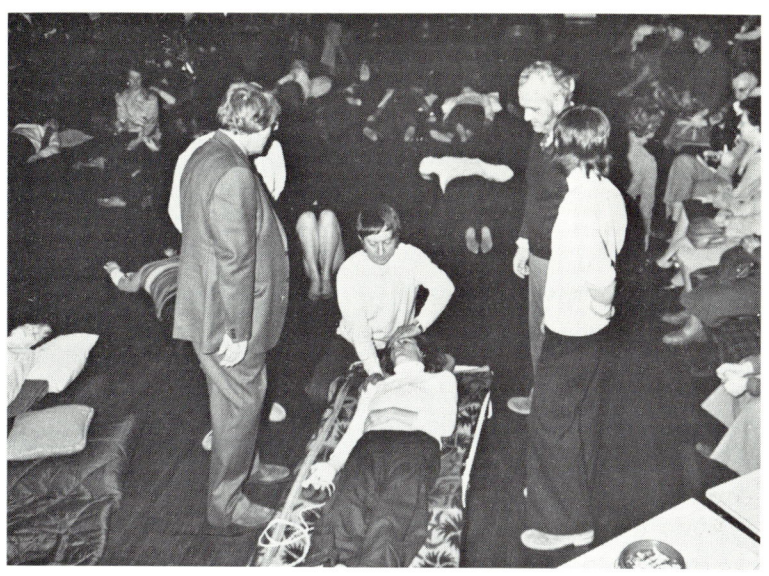

Cain treats a close friend, who is in a deeply recorded trance, at a public demonstration.

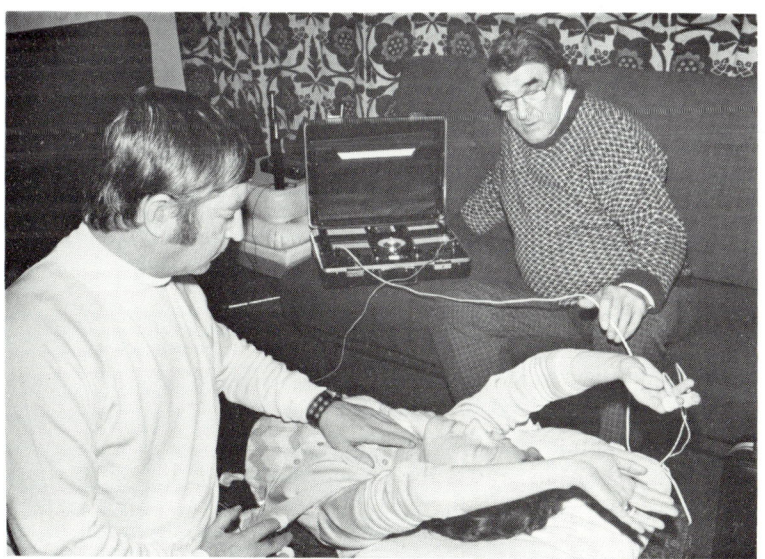

Scientific researcher Angus McHutchon tests a patient's trance state for the Society of Psychical Research in England.

her stomach as the other worked slowly down her spinal column. Opening his eyes, Cain was flabbergasted to find the girl bent right over from the waist, her head nearly touching the floor. He felt he had been in trance, probably for the first time.

From then on the mysterious manipulations began with a boy suffering from muscular dystrophy. Cain, amazed, was able to step away to watch the boy's wasted limbs jerk into unaccustomed movements as his spirit world helpers masterminded the entire process. Later the power creating these bizarre conditions progressively grew stronger, with some patients seemingly flung around the small sanctuary, but never coming to any harm despite the violent movements. Once a 15-stone man, seated on a stool, moved several feet towards Cain without any visible means of propulsion.

Sceptics theorised that Cain was using hypnosis techniques to cause these manifestations. Though he readily admits he has the ability to hypnotise, it is clear on watching him at work that the trance state entered into by his patients is not induced by suggestive tactics. Cain merely sits at a patient's side, his eyes closed as he goes into the healing silence, passively offering himself for the spirit healers to function through. The sufferer's eyes do not see Cain's face. No words or commands are uttered. He does not usually even touch the patient. His hands are suspended an inch or so above the person's head. Time after time the comatose state is induced in this way.

It was inevitable that scientists and parapsychologists, those Doubting Thomas' of the paranormal, should begin to take an active interest in Cain and his amazing physical phenomena. Cain is willing to be investigated under controlled laboratory conditions by any reputable scientist, as well as being prepared to travel to any foreign country to demonstrate his spiritual gifts. Japanese researchers tested him twice in Tokyo in 1976. He has undergone laboratory tests by mathematician Prof John Taylor of King's College, London.

Cain was elated when the brilliant scientist accepted his offer to become his first 'healer guinea pig.' With him at one test session were Angus McHutchon, a research and development executive, and George Newton, a solicitor, both of Southport, Merseyside. McHutchon is a Society for Psychical Research member. He and Newton belong to the Merseyside Parapsychology Society.

They watched Taylor make cardiograph records of Cain. The

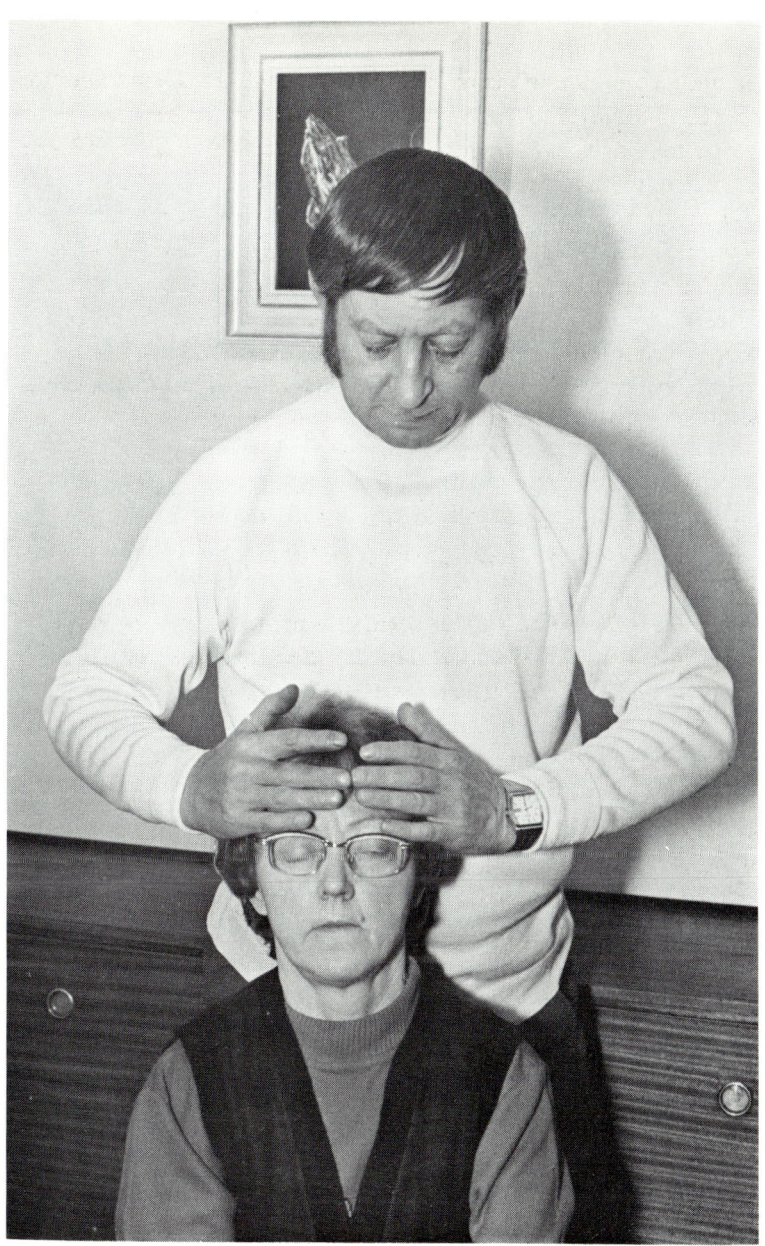

Elizabeth Heffy of Birkenhead wished she had known of Cain years earlier. She says she would have been rescued from needless years of pain.

scientist told the party the abnormal feature of his initial tests was that Cain's heart rate was five times higher than normal.

McHutchon, who has tested Cain in his sanctuary, says: 'We have proved he definitely goes into trance. We have measured this on our instruments.' While treating Tony Woodcock, 40, of Birkenhead, who has osteo-arthritis, McHutchon's oscilloscope also showed the healer's heartbeat nearly five times higher than the patient's. Most of the arthritis in Woodcock's head, shoulders, back, left and right hips and knees had dissipated in five months.

McHutchon observed Cain to see what happens during healing. His tests concluded that when he goes into trance his patients fall into an altered state of consciousness. While Cain treated a muscular dystrophy patient, his sensitive equipment recorded three significant tremors. They were synchronised between healer and patient. They lasted only a second which, says McHutchon, means there is a direct contact between the two without speech.

Intriguing tests were conducted during absent healing, with which Cain has had outstanding success. Patients and observers were in a house in Formby, Lancs. McHutchon and Newton monitored Cain. One experiment was designed to check whether he could diagnose an unidentified girl's condition. She was troubled by intense pain after an ovarian cysts operation, which had been badly performed. Cain was asked to diagnose from a distance the cause of her pain. All he could pick up psychically was 'a cut too near the right.'

When the researchers returned to Formby the girl said her right side had adhesions and excessive scar tissue. In a further experiment Cain was hypnotised by McHutchon. A patient reported a tingling sensation and being 'beautifully relaxed' when Cain was both diagnosing and healing him.

Adds McHutchon: 'We have proved scientifically that altered states of consciousness occur in the patient while Cain is healing. My conclusion is that he and his patients go into trance when there is rapport between them. We have to delve deeper than this to discover the actual mechanics of healing. We need to probe the brain rhythms.'

Newton, whose legal profession background has trained him to assess evidence, has no doubt that healing takes place with Cain. His association with Cain started after the healer contacted Liverpool University and was referred to the Merseyside Parapsychology

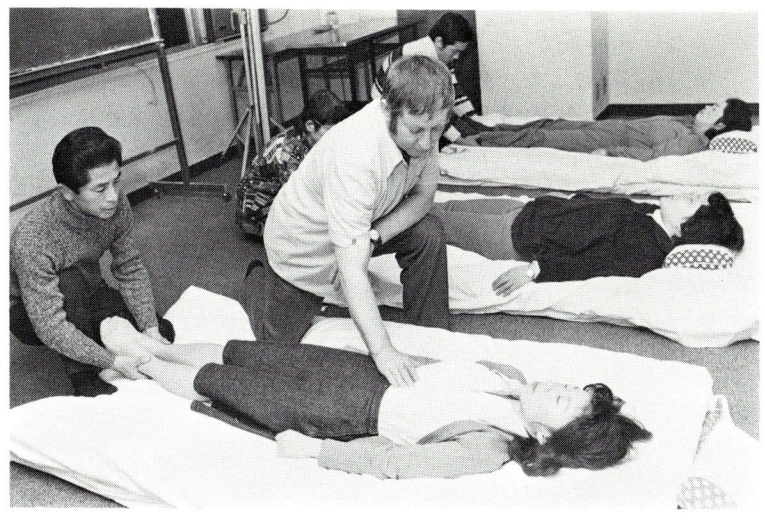

On his second successful visit to Japan, Cain instructed would-be healers in his methods. Here he shows how patients go into a comatose state.

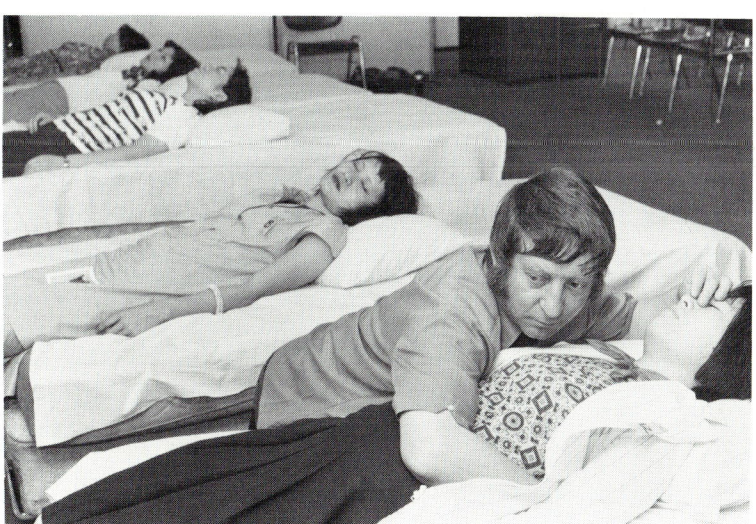

Five patients in a row are seen as John Cain gives treatment. The patient second from the right has Cain's photograph in her lap.

Society. 'A good report of Cain was given. We arranged to observe his healing work. Results have fully justified our interest. They are even better than we expected,' Newton says.

'Call healing what you will, magnetic or spiritual. But our analysis shows there is a solid, proven foundation for it. The changes that take place between healer and patient are obviously significant and demand greater scientific study. Now we have to find out what happens in the healing process. We need to make a more sophisticated investigation with the most up-to-date and expensive instruments that can be obtained.'

CHAPTER 3

WOMAN IS 'REBORN'

ONE of Cain's prize patients – she regards him almost as a guru and with good reason cites him as the world's greatest psychic healer – is vivacious Sheila Mitchell, 34, of Clifton Avenue, Eastham. She was a pitiable psoriasis victim at the age of $4\frac{1}{2}$. This distressing complaint begins as a dry crust of skin. It gradually thickens and spreads round the body. The scaly white crust can be sliced with a razor blade.

Sheila was covered from head to foot. The unpleasant treatment consists of scraping with cold tar ointment. She used to scream when she was little, but gradually became inured to the terrible condition. Doctors had to concede defeat. After 30 years she had not improved. There was nothing more they could do. As invariably happens after a no-hope medical verdict, a sufferer turns in final desperation to spirit healing.

Sheila found herself treading Cain's well-worn path. She had no faith whatsoever. It was a last throw of the dice. She was then 30. Behind her lay a disease-ruined childhood and she was resigned to her adult life going the same way. But after nine months at Cain's healing hands she was completely cured. Even the healer was surprised at so rapid a success. He had tentatively forecast betterment in two years because the disease was so deep-seated.

John Cain, the animal lover, pictured with pet Labrador, Nigger, aged eighteen, whom he cured of blindness.

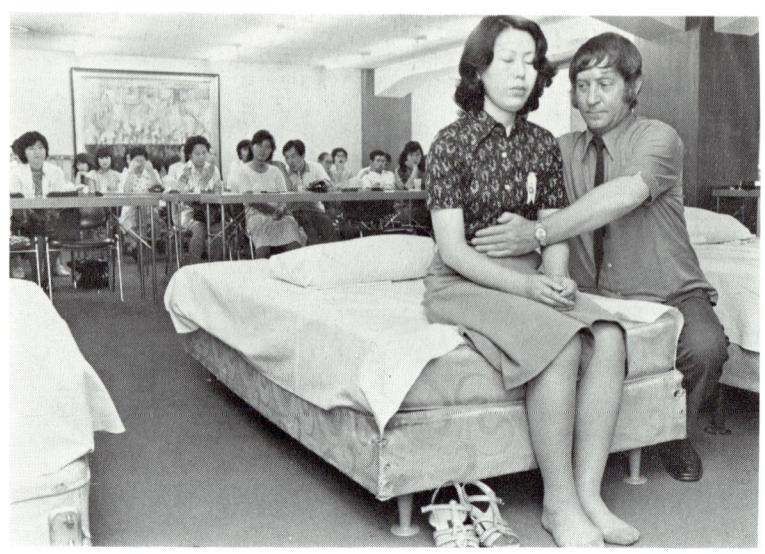

Japanese observers watch intently as the British healer concentrates on a sufferer's stomach condition.

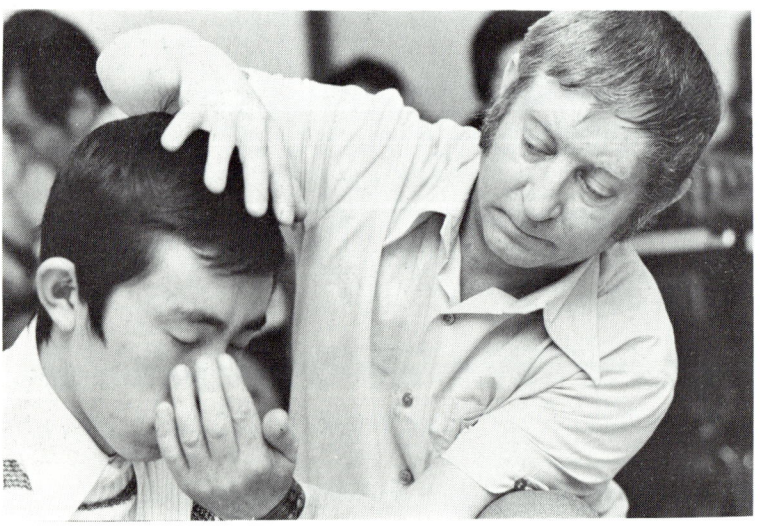

Here the healer treats a stubborn nasal complaint during his Tokyo demonstrations when he was besieged by hundreds of sufferers.

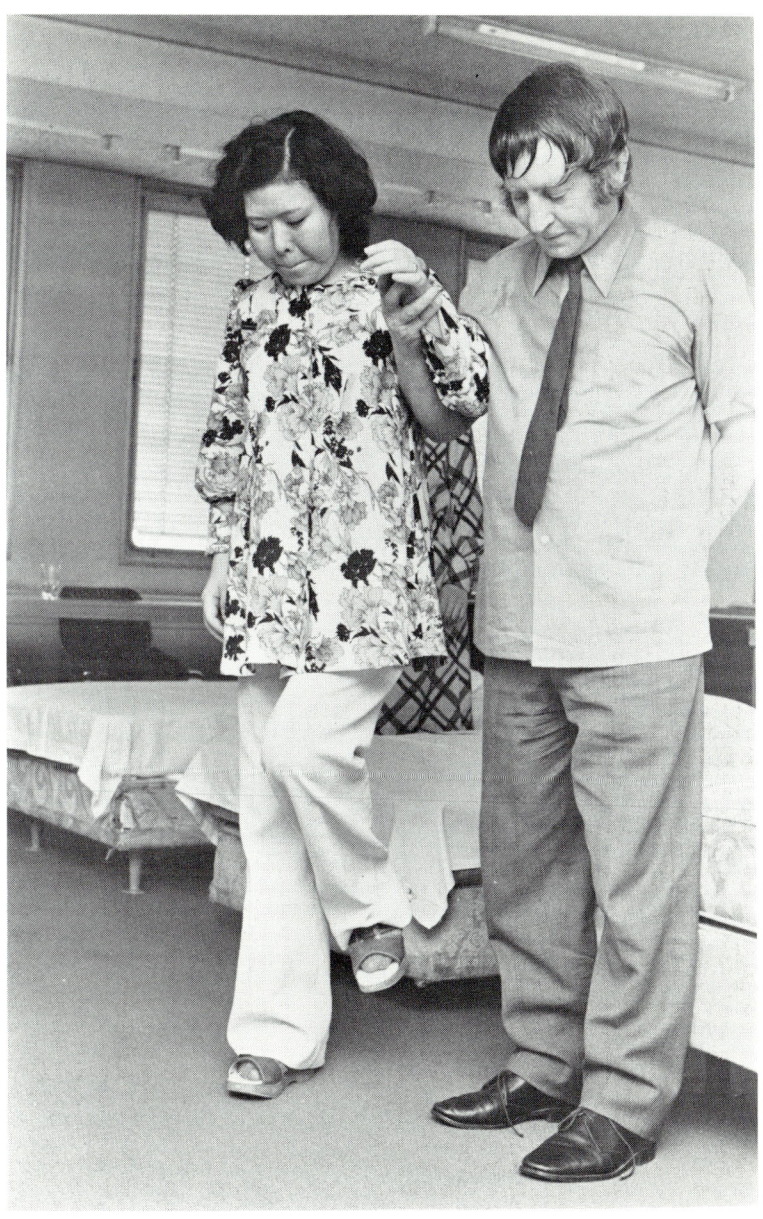

A Japanese rheumatoid arthritis sufferer walks without crutches for the first time after a Cain Healing Demonstration in Tokyo in 1976.

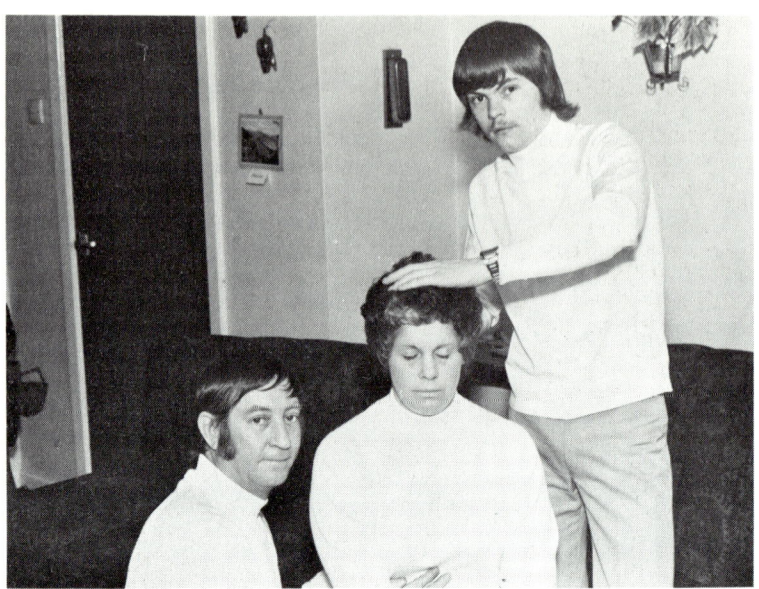

Cain's son John helps Sheila Mitchell relax in an upright position before healing begins.

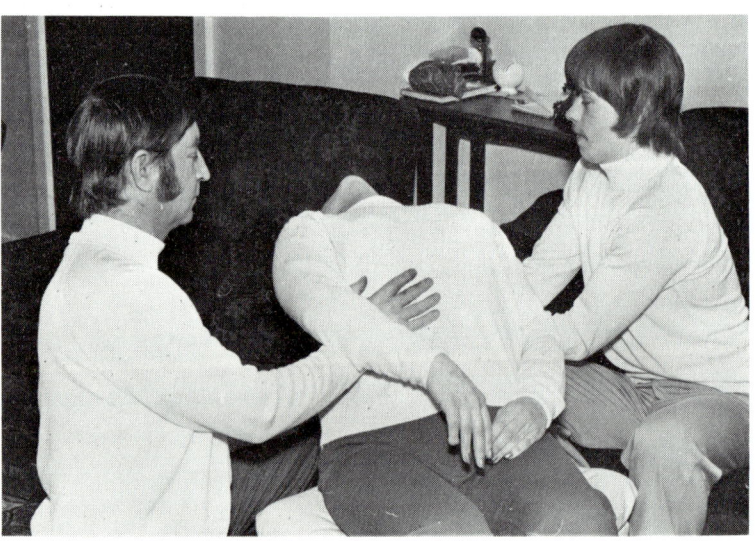

Sheila Mitchell, who was cured of a distressing skin allergy which defied the best medical brains, slumps back into a coma after Cain and his son John junior lay on hands.

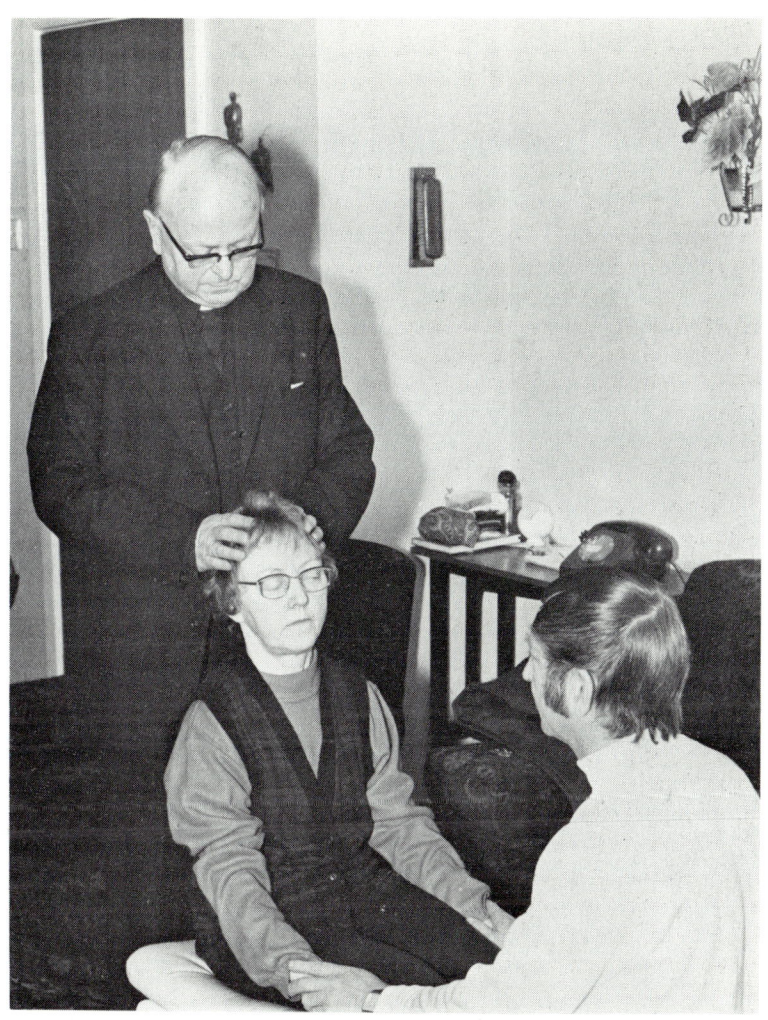

Unitarian Minister, The Rev. William Stribley, helps Cain heal a sufferer. He is an extraordinary Cain devotee.

The condition suddenly flared again after her mother had an illness. Again Cain made her blemish-free. Today Sheila is a new woman. She calls herself 'reborn. It's fantastic to be able to venture into shops to try clothes on. This is one of those feminine luxuries I could never enjoy before I met John Cain. I owe him everything.' She read about his healing powers in a local newspaper. His surname attracted her. It was the same as that of a girl she knew years ago. She decided it must be an omen.

Her condition began to improve immediately. She was overjoyed. In the healing trance she goes back to the time her psoriasis started. Cain's guide, Carl, has spoken to her. 'He said I had to be very patient. I was taken back to when I was a small child, even to when I was inside my mother's womb.' Later a local priest, learning of her frequent visits to a spirit healer, admonished her saying she would have to choose between the Church and Cain. She remarked, to the clergyman's astonishment, 'Through John Cain, and not the Church, I have had my faith in God restored!' Apart from the disease, Cain also cured her of asthma and bronchitis.

To observe Sheila in a typical healing demonstration is an incredible experience. Without being touched or spoken to she quickly slips into a deep trance. Then her inert body galvanises into action as the unseen manipulators put her through an extraordinary series of meticulous, complicated exercises worthy of a highly-trained athlete, which Sheila most certainly is not. Normally a person undergoing such rigorous, muscular movements would feel supple. But Sheila's legs feel heavy and rigid, like steel rods. It seems impossible to make an indentation in her flesh.

She slips to the floor and contorts herself into advanced yoga postures. She has never studied the art and, before her supernormal lessons began in Cain's sanctuary, she couldn't even have done ordinary PT. Amazingly, after more than 30 minutes' non-stop contortions, her breathing rate seemed little more than normal, as though she had done nothing more energetic than walking her dog. Next her feet pounded the pale blue sanctuary wall in a bewilderingly fast flurry.

Apart from her own remarkable recovery, Sheila joyously relates how a hospital's doctors regarded her mother's return from a 'no hope' coma as a 'miracle.' What Sheila did not tell them was that she acted as Cain's 'agent' to treat her mother, Harriet, 67.

This intriguing story began when Sheila found Harriet had collapsed. She was rushed to hospital. A distraught Sheila was told, 'There is no hope.' But she, too, had been termed medically hopeless till Cain proved otherwise. She told him about Harriet's plight, asking for distant healing. When her mother pulled through the coma, which the doctors did not expect to happen, Sheila's hopes rose.

Again she appealed to the ever-ready Cain. This time he suggested she act as his agent by giving 'proxy' treatment at the bedside. 'I did this. The results were electrifying. My hands seemed to be directed to various areas of my mother's body. It certainly didn't seem like me manipulating her. I knew it was spirit healing power at work. The hospital room became very hot, just as it does in the healer's sanctuary. Several times I went into trance while giving this strange treatment. When Mother regained consciousness fully she had no control over her body. She was unable to speak.'

Sheila reported progress to Cain by telephone each day. He instructed his 'agent' to concentrate on certain body areas. She dutifully did as directed. To her astonishment her mother's speech returned. A feature of the remarkable healing that impressed Sheila is that Harriet received psychic injections. 'I have seen so much of Cain's work I knew this happened. When she came out of the coma her legs were jerking. She remarked she felt as though people had been sticking needles in her. She actually thought she was having injections. But there was no nurse in the vicinity at those times. I knew without any vestige of doubt that it was spirit healing at work.'

Mother and daughter are Roman Catholics. Since Harriet's dramatic recovery she has been told about Cain's remarkable intercession and Sheila's enthusiastic role in it. Says Sheila: 'She believes it totally. She is thankful to have made a full recovery. The hospital staff claimed her case as a miracle. How could I begin to explain it had been a proxy healing? In that sense, I would certainly describe it as a "miracle".'

So devoted is she to Cain's work, Sheila would like to develop as a healer. The incident with her mother was the first time she had tried to treat through Cain. 'It was a fantastic experience. He is a truly remarkable man.'

A sequel to the story is that the healing seems to have corrected a serious heart defect. Explains Sheila: 'Mother used to suffer heart attacks. Since the episode in hospital she has had a medical check-up and her heart declared to be in marvellous condition.'

CHAPTER 4

CLERIC CALLS HIM 'AMAZING'

ONE of Cain's most impressed and vociferous supporters is a clergyman. The Rev Bill Stribley, 63, Minister of the West Kirby Unitarian Free Christian Church, Wirral, with which he combines the ministry of the Matthew Henry Chapel, Blacon, Cheshire, testifies to the ex-blacksmith's extraordinary ability. At first sceptical about the claims attributed to Cain, Stribley had the courage to investigate for himself. He was 'richly rewarded' by witnessing remarkable phenomena.

Soon after taking his post at Blacon in 1972, he was intrigued to hear that a local woman was said to have been healed of cancer by Cain. In gratitude she had thrown open her flat on Monday evenings for Cain to use as a healing sanctuary. Stribley thought it would be interesting to see what it was all about.

'I was incredulous about the woman's alleged healing. Cure of cancer? On the surface it seemed hard to credit. Yet I went to investigate with an open mind. Unitarians are interested in all religions. We would never discredit other faiths. We feel there is one God, but that there are many ways to reach him. We certainly do not say that Christianity is the only way to achieve this. By that same token I would never decry Spiritualism, though I had no association with it before meeting John Cain.'

Stribley's determination to try to understand Cain's reputed powers was boosted by Ray Cumin, the treasurer of Stribley's Church scout group. He described the healer as 'marvellous.' When Stribley was invited to a demonstration he accepted with alacrity. What he did not know then was that Cumin, a healer in his own right, assisted Cain in his work.

What did the cleric expect to find? 'I visualised a fast-talking, high-pressure type businessman who would make suggestions to people with the right kind of receptive mind to enable them to believe and have faith that they would be helped. I could, for example, readily understand some types of mental illness being helped greatly in the presence of a forceful, perhaps hypnotic, personality.' But his preconceived notions were quickly and dramatically shattered. He was immediately impressed by Cain's obvious dedication and sincerity in his humane approach.

'I found him to be a most modest, quiet and humble man who said very little indeed to patients. He certainly did not employ auto-suggestive practices in any form. There was no way in which he could be utilising hypnosis. I saw several people obviously greatly helped the evening I attended his 'surgery,' the first time I had seen him work.'

Having been hugely impressed, Stribley attended many more Cain demonstrations in the next six months. Each one convinced him more of the 'amazing successes of his treatments. Principally rheumatic patients seemed to respond, and certainly those with mental problems.'

Then Stribley invited Cain to give a healing demonstration at the Matthew Henry Chapel, Blacon. The church committee offered no objections. Stribley advertised the event in a local newspaper. As it was a somewhat radical move, the minister thought he should explain to his regular parishioners what was happening. He begged them to attend, describing some of the healing cases he had seen.

The result was a packed church. 'They all came. There was not one dissenter. I was proud of my flock that night. They had displayed tolerance, not hostility, to something they perhaps did not understand. Their attitude was a heartening religious object lesson for all creeds.'

Later Stribley even helped Cain by laying on hands with him to increase the spirit power for healing. He was surprised to find himself 'almost in a trance.'

At the service, which included hymns and prayers, Stribley asked those who had been treated by Cain to stand up. About 20 responded. He suggested they should not volunteer to receive treatment because he was anxious to see the result on people who had never experienced spirit healing before.

'After the laying on of hands many expressed later their joy over being cured of various ailments, including a hospital nursing sister who had suffered migraine for many years. I have been in touch with her since. In the following 12 months she had had only one slight attack, whereas before the healing she had them each week. Naturally being a trained nurse she was quite sceptical at first about Cain's supernormal ability to help her condition. But, again naturally, after the dramatic result of her first treatment she changed her mind. Now she advises many other unfortunates to seek Cain's aid.'

So impressed was he by Cain that Stribley, an ordained minister since 1971 but previously a Methodist Church lay preacher for 36 years, with remarkable frankness says: 'It would not be unthinkable for me to embrace Spiritualism. And my present congregation (at Blacon) would not criticise me for so doing.'

CHAPTER 5

CRIPPLE'S 'MIRACLE' CURE

THE day after his momentous church healing service Stribley was unexpectedly involved in yet another Cain spectacular, this time resulting in a healing that still has this bluff, wholly likeable cleric shaking his head in utter disbelief.

He took his car for service to a local garage. The mechanic, who did not belong to any church or recognised religion, asked how things were going at Stribley's church. This prompted him to relate Cain's amazing spirit healing demonstration the previous evening. The mechanic looked thoughtful. Then he said it was a pity it had not been a week later for his mother had a friend visiting from Norfolk who had been severely crippled with arthritis for many years and was also deaf.

Stribley replied that he was confident he could arrange for Cain to treat her, but would rather the request for help came from the sufferer. He suggested that the mechanic should mention the healer on her arrival. Some days later the mechanic telephoned Stribley to say his mother's friend, a woman, would very much appreciate seeing Cain. Subsequently Cain went to the woman in Blacon.

Stribley accompanied him. Graphically he describes the remarkable scenes that followed:

'I was amazed to see how badly crippled the woman was. Her husband and a friend had to help her from the kitchen into the lounge and into a chair. She could not walk unaided. Cain asked me to open with a short prayer, laying my hands with his on the patient's head.

'Within a few minutes he suggested that the patient stand and walk. Having seen the help she needed to move, this seemed quite impossible. To my astonishment, however, she walked briskly round the room, down some steps into the kitchen and back up again before bursting into unrestrained tears of joy. It was an intensely emotional spectacle.

'Everybody was absolutely speechless and could describe the transformation only as a miracle. I was flabbergasted. I didn't really think for one minute that Cain could make any impression on her, such was the gravity of her condition. It was firmly in my mind before the healing began that a miracle would have to occur for any improvement to happen.'

Two days later the woman rang Stribley to say that she was still mobile, that there had been no deterioration. As she was returning home next day she felt she would like to see Cain again to receive what she called a 'booster.' This time she attended his home sanctuary, and again Stribley was a fascinated onlooker.

Upon laying on of hands she immediately lapsed into a comatose state. Recovering, she announced that she felt 'absolutely wonderful.' Cain instructed her to remove her hearing aid, suggesting she no longer needed it.

'To my amazement,' says Stribley, 'I discovered she could hear a watch ticking. In utter delight she stuffed the hearing aid into her handbag.'

The sad feature is that, having been the recipient of brilliant spirit healing, the woman ungraciously refused to identify herself for Cain's records and so that follow through checks could be made to establish whether her cure remained permanent. She also flatly rejected the idea of having herself photographed with Cain and Stribley as a pictorial reminder of an outstanding event.

Cain asked her to drop a line to let him know how she got on. To the amazement of Cain and Stribley, she replied that she would neither give her name nor address. She didn't want these published in case she received correspondence from other sufferers with which she would find it impossible to cope. She asked Stribley if he thought she was being unreasonable.

'I had to reply that I most certainly did and told her if I had received such a wonderful, inspiring healing I shouldn't care where my name and address was published. I should be only too pleased to give encouragement to other sufferers who might then be shown the way to similar benefit. Despite this she remained unmoved. It was an extraordinary reaction.

'However, the garage mechanic, with whom I am still in touch, but who also will not supply the woman's name and address, tells me she is still perfectly well. Long before the healing she had had her driving licence rescinded as she was unfit to be in charge of a motor vehicle. But since the treatment she had passed her driving test again and was back on the road.'

Stribley calls it the most miraculous spontaneous healing he has seen. 'Even now, two years after it happened, I find it difficult to believe that I saw that terribly bent arthritic's body straighten and her clenched fingers become normal.'

His wife, Marjorie, was staggered to find the woman's hearing had been restored. 'I had never seen anything like it before.'

Stribley says: 'How can I, as a minister of religion, discredit this kind of wonderful, God-given healing? When Jesus was on earth he told his disciples to preach the Gospel and to heal the sick. Ministers have been so busy writing their sermons they have forgotten to execute his ministrations about healing the sick.

'In this case I call it God working through Cain. I am interested only in results. I told myself it would be wicked not to testify to this man's achievements. He must be a God-fearing man to be used in that way. Clearly God believes in him. Spiritualism's phenomena are something you have to see. Are you to tell lies when you witness such healing miracles?

'I am only too pleased that I am coming to live nearer to Cain so that I may be able to see even more of his inspiring work.'

Stribley loses no opportunity of sending the stricken to Cain for his able results. An agnostic, unemployable because he was crippled, had returned to work completely cured.

'We have to admit there is some wonderful healing power coming from somewhere, from God or the spirit world. It's all one and the same to me,' Stribley smiles.

CHAPTER 6

'DEAD' MASTER GIVES CAIN LESSON

STRIBLEY also plays a corroboratory part in another of the extraordinary catalogue of physical phenomena attending Cain's healing sessions.

Judo expert Cain (status: second Dan Belt) was startled to find himself being put into judo holds while treating a woman with arthritis. He experienced this eerie phenomenon a year earlier for the first time. Treating a patient who had suffered a stroke, he experienced a series of hand-technique 'throws'.

But the arthritic woman, unwittingly being used in a unique two-world contest, tested Cain's judo techniques to the utmost. Manifesting through her was a high-ranking judo expert of sixth Dan grade. After giving treatment, Cain extended his hand.

'Suddenly I was gripped. A complete wrist lock was exerted on both hands. Then followed a series of intricate judo techniques. Startled, I began to speak in judo terms to the entity controlling the woman. I am convinced he was a Japanese master under whom I trained. He was national coach for the British Judo Association.'

Cain trained under him at a summer school at Liverpool University in 1951. Now, in his sanctuary, using an entranced woman crippled with arthritis, the old master had returned to see how well Cain had learned his lessons!

In Japanese Cain told his unseen adversary: ' "If it is you, I will counter with a foot trip." As I swept my foot it was countered almost as soon as I touched my patient's foot. It was fantastic. It was an amazing discarnate judo lesson!

'I then said I would pretend to apply a strangle hold. This manoeuvre was again immediately and effectively countered. I was nearly taken over the patient's head. If there had been room I would have been thrown. It was a most gentle, almost caressing, movement. The only man I know with such skill was my Japanese tutor. He committed suicide in London 17 years ago.'

The dramatic encounter lasted 45 minutes. Cain used all his considerable judo experience to work out moves. But he was effortlessly countered.

'Each time I was taken off my balance. Though somewhat eerie, it was a fantastic experience grappling with an unseen adversary.'

Stribley was intrigued when he heard about the strange judo contest. With two independent witnesses, one a parapsychologist, the other an electronics expert, he decided to investigate 'this extraordinary manifestation.'

He watched Cain treat a middle-aged woman. 'She went into a comatose state, then gripped Cain in a series of complicated judo holds which he was powerless to resist. At times he was thrown about the room. Once he was literally hurled against the opposite wall.'

Stribley and the others were riveted by the spectacle of the two-world combat. At the end the patient's wrists were freed from a previously locked state.

The cleric adds: 'It would appear therefore that we had not only witnessed a judo expert manifesting through the patient, but healing taking place simultaneously. All this must sound difficult to believe. But I feel I must report that the independent witnesses and I were greatly impressed. I am happy to testify to what I saw at this fascinating session.'

Another witness to the enthralling contest is Ray Cumin, Cain's healing assistant. He and Cain want the judo phenomenon demonstrated under strictly controlled test conditions. Cain is 'fairly certain' that it could be demonstrated, though it has happened so far only twice.

'The actual throws could take place, but clearly it's not the kind of incident that could be produced to order.'

The woman patient, who did not realise the 'dead' Japanese controlled her to join 'battle' with Cain, said later she 'felt powerful' during the session.

Coincidentally, a fortnight earlier a medium friend received clairvoyance about Cain. She told him later he has had a Japanese guide with him since birth. He confirmed he had been given this information several times by other psychics.

He has noted a distinct pattern in that all the physical manifestations through his patients represent activities he has followed. At 12 he was a yoga enthusiast. During healing in the trance state many of his patients do yoga exercises, though in most cases the movements are completely alien.

At other times his guide will encourage a bad arthritic case to dance. Cain used to be a ballroom fanatic for 15 years as a young man. Occasionally some patients go through the motions of ordinary physical training exercises. Cain was, of course, an Army PT instructor.

He poses the questions: 'Whether these unusual side-effects are part of my healing development, I don't know. Could these results be triggered from my subconscious mind? Again, who can say?'

Whatever the answer to the intriguing questions, certainly no one can complain that Cain's healing sessions lack 'atmosphere'.

CHAPTER 7

VICAR CALLS IT 'GOD-GIVEN GIFT'

YET another clergyman readily sings the praises of Cain's superb healing touch. The Rev Peter Fowles, Anglican vicar of Towin, near Rhyl, North Wales, clearly has a happier marriage because of spirit healing.

Excruciating pain for nearly three years caused by nerve pressure to muscles in her left arm brought his wife, Jean, to the sanctuary after orthodox medicine could provide no relief. Two examinations in London hospitals left doctors in a quandary, and Jean still with her agony.

Fowles heard about Cain through a friend. In his case he was not sceptical about spirit healing. 'I came believing,' he says. 'In each of us there is an element of healing capability. Some form of the gift is latent in most people. In Cain especially it is exceptionally noticeable. I have been very impressed by him. If we hadn't believed in healing we couldn't have come because it would have been hypocrisy.'

His overriding fear, which was quickly banished, was that Cain might prove to be one of those who crudely exercise a mental predominance over other people rather than displaying a God-given

41

gift. Fowles is convinced Cain falls into that last category. Thousands of others believe so, too.

Jean talks with pleasure about the healing. On her first four visits she fell into trance. 'It surprised me because I didn't know what to expect. It was a pleasantly relaxing experience. Then I noticed that my shoulder pain was beginning to recede. The pain had had a gradual wearing-down effect. It was so severe that after three years of having so many tablets a nasty reaction developed. It was frightening.'

After Cain's treatment started she began to get complete periods without pain, 'which was wonderful. Now I am fine. I have to take care I do not try to lift heavy objects. If I forget – and when you are pain-free it is easy to do so – the pain will return.' Then a further session with Cain's magical hands puts her right again.

Fowles says: 'While she is not completely cured, she is able now to control her condition. She still gets pain if she misbehaves.'

His contact with Cain has brought him a new interest. 'I knew of the Rosicrucian movement which flourished in the 16th century and broke out in America in the 1800's. This type of organisation does not impress me. But the work that Cain and people like him do does impress me greatly.'

His son, Paul, 12, is also being treated by Cain for sinus trouble. Says Fowles, 'It is difficult to explain in words the joy we have experienced in finding a spiritual gift as personified by Cain.'

* * *

PATIENT Laura Lawler of Napier Drive, Moreton, Wirral, was crestfallen when John cancelled appointments to visit Canada in July, 1976. But, as he told all his patients, he assured her the healing would continue automatically in his absence. This is absent treatment which sufferers all over the world can link up to by focussing attention mentally on Cain or, preferably, on his photograph.

One night while he was abroad, Laura took his picture to a church service. At 7 p.m., when Cain's healing circle sits to radiate treatment, she felt her toes twitching as though invisible hands manipulated them. Glancing at the photograph, she was astonished to see a distinct blue haze surrounding it.

When five diphtheria left Laura with partially paralysed legs, spine and hands. She had bones set by surgery. She went to a Harry

Edwards meeting, 'looking for the miracle which never seemed to come.' She kept seeing stories about Cain. She 'knew' he was the one she had to reach.

Cain, who makes no promises, didn't think he could help her. The paralysis was too set. But the beneficial change he wrought has created a different woman. Before meeting Cain she was terribly depressed and never had time for others. Often she felt suicidal. Now people stop her to remark on her dramatic change.

'Today, thanks to Cain, I am a happy soul with a renewed purpose in life. Healing has given me such an uplift. I have become a new woman.'

Laura is convinced that but for her contact with Cain she would have been an accident victim, seriously injured if not dead. Faced by an oncoming car near a pedestrian crossing, she knew she could not get out of its way by her own means. In the split seconds it took for the drama to unfold, she resigned herself to the inevitable.

'Then I felt pressure on my shoulder as though being pushed by an invisible hand.' And the car brushed her stomach instead of hitting her squarely.

Laura is also developing clairvoyance since coming into the healer's influence. She 'saw' a Japanese girl, Mount Fuji and an aeroplane. A week later, Cain, out of the blue, was invited to visit Japan.

* * *

SOME people find themselves tortured by conventional religious scruples when deciding whether to go to a spirit healer. Such was the case with Barbara Radcliffe, 35, of Connah's Quay, Clwyd, North Wales.

She was desperately worried about son Jamie, ten, an asthma sufferer since birth. He was six before she realised it was a permanent condition. All specialists could do was to prescribe drugs.

A clergyman told her to try Cain. The idea disturbed her. 'I used to go to church and think, "What the devil am I doing sitting here?" I felt guilty. I was in a dreadful dilemma. Then I didn't go to church for about four years. I found growing interest in Spiritualism and healing. I devoured library books on its philosophy.'

The upshot was that, after four years of tortured doubt, she took Jamie to Cain. After five treatments his improvement was remarkable.

'His chest is clear. It is definitely a cure. Cain is working on his nasal problem. It is already much better.'

Barbara is also amazed by her own healing. She wore eye glasses since puberty and always suffered chest trouble. She was forced to use dark glasses to shield her eyes from normal light. Sometimes she even had to wear them to bed.

Soon after Cain began treating her she told a friend, 'These glasses are annoying me.' She removed them, despite the brilliant sunshine that day. She has never needed them since. Previously her social life had been strictly limited.

'I couldn't go to pubs or parties. Smoke-filled rooms would play havoc with my eyes. I had to go to bed because I couldn't watch television. I daren't wear mascara. Now I can watch TV, go to smoke-filled parties and wear mascara.'

When Cain treated her she felt a pressure on her eyes as though she were falling into deep unconsciousness.

CHAPTER 8

ATTACKING THE HUMBUG

CAIN, always the direct, forthright Northerner, whose homespun philosophy and innate bluntness, so reminiscent of the old-time smithy, have not exactly endeared him to Spiritualism's top hierarchy, is clearly more at home in his natural healing environment. His role is far removed from Spiritualism's squabbling centre. He has set the proverbial cat among the pigeons more than once when attending functions at Stansted Hall, Essex, headquarters of the Spiritualists' National Union.

Cain enjoys puncturing egos and tilting at those in authority, who strut and pontificate, blissfully unaware that they alienate ever larger sections of the movement. If Spiritualism's edifices should ever totter and crumble, it is heartening to know that its main work and ideals will continue as personified by the healer in his home sanctuary, the humble church and the dedicated back-street worker who seek only to serve humanity. This is why Cain and many like him are bitterly opposed to the kind of humbug which is so prevalent in Spiritualism today. It is why Cain seldom talks about Spiritualism or that he is a Spiritualist. His job is to serve the spirit world and this is what he has dedicated his life to do. Only someone with such total conviction and resolute determination could spend up to 12 hours a day, seven days a week in a small, dark room trying to heal a pitiable assortment of usually medically-incurable people, using only his hands, the outlet for spirit power. Who today would have the courage to throw up a secure business, with all the material niceties of life, and become virtually housebound because a 'dead' father says, 'Heal, my son!' On that basis alone, Cain has to be someone very special.

He is not a religious man and does not 'mess about' with herbs or medicines. 'I just hold my hands or press gently on the site of a pain and concentrate with a kind of prayer. Not to God as the Church represent him, but to the supernormal power in which I believe.'

One of Cain's first patients was medium Alan Crossley who lives in Chester, about six miles from Cain. Crossley has been interested in the occult for about 30 years and is a noted authority on the subject. He told Cain of severe pain he had experienced for some time through a slipped disc. He appealed for healing.

'He did so, literally placing his finger on the "hot spot" – and that was that. I have not had the slightest trouble since.'

Then Crossley's wife suffered a cerebral hemorrhage and was admitted to Clatterbridge Hospital, Cheshire. Afer X-rays and examination Crossley was told by a hospital doctor that no assurance could be given of any definite recovery. In fact, if there was to be one it would take a very long time.

'I asked Cain if he would accompany me to the hospital. For three nights he simply held my wife's hand. Then her speech returned. Seven days later she was discharged. No drugs or medical treatment had been administered. Both the hospital sister and the senior consultant expressed amazement at the recovery, which the latter described as "remarkable".'

Crossley, naturally, was fascinated by Cain's spiritual healing powers. He watched the list of cures grow. He marvelled as he saw a woman with a frozen shoulder, unable to lift her arm, even after lengthy medical treatment, raise it straight above her head after one visit.

'I am not gullible,' says Crossley. 'I have seen too many quacks and cranks posing as mediums, clairvoyants and healers, to be taken in easily. I feel beyond doubt that Cain, probably through his intense preoccupation and concentration upon the occult, has developed latent powers which we cannot fully understand, but which perhaps all of us possess and which, one day, will be used as commonly as we take an aspirin today.'

Sheila Scott, 24, a computer operator of Hurst Avenue, Sale, Cheshire, is another who gratefully acknowledges Cain's remarkable powers in saying, 'I have a lot to thank spirit healing for.' She has the rare medical condition of sustemic lupus emytosous nephroic syndrome which causes diseased joints and internal organs. It was diagnosed in 1973. Shortly after giving birth to a daughter, Sheila's kidneys collapsed. She was rushed to hospital. She had a biopsy and the disease was discovered. She had steroids treatment.

In desperation, Sheila's mother wrote to Harry Edwards. 'From the day he received the letter the tablets started working.' This encouraged her to seek help from local church healers. Her condition stayed steady.

Then she read about Cain and made an appointment. After just four treatments her hospital doctors said 'they didn't think I could have done so well and were very pleased with my progress. My blood pressure became normal. I also now have far more energy and I lead a perfectly normal life.'

Sheila's mother has also benefited, this time from Cain's absent healing. 'She has suffered with ulcers for 15 years and has been in terrible pain. She has held Cain's picture during absent healing and the pain has ceased.'

CHAPTER 9

THEIR MISERY ENDS

THE strange phenomena attributed to Cain's healing sessions are recounted graphically by Mrs Joan Nicholls of Chester Road, Ellesmere Port, Cheshire.

An arthritic sufferer since December, 1967, when she was 48, she received what she calls 'wonderful hospital treatment.' But 1974 was a bad year for her. In March, 1975, she first visited Cain, 'after much deliberation. I came open-minded, neither believing nor disbelieving. I was in a very sorry state, bent over, hands hooked. I had to be fed, washed, dressed and then put into a chair. I had to wait for somebody to come in to see to me during the day.'

Nothing seemed to happen for the first few healings in Cain's sanctuary. But gradually she felt benefit.

'I go into the trance state. From what I am told I am manipulated, though I remember nothing. I have tried to repeat these manipulations of my own free-will, but they do not happen. While in trance I have been to some fantastic places.'

Once on recovering from trance Joan was 'literally frozen solid for three days. The coldness went and I had a good spell with little pain. My movements improved.'

In September, 1976, she had a 'remarkable experience. After healing I was once again frozen. My husband took me home. I felt very ill. I was put to bed. Still feeling frozen I entered my quiet period. My knees swelled to the size of large dinner plates. It was horrifying. Later I began to perspire. It was not ordinary perspiration. Water poured from my entire body. My hair was wet through. As this happened you could see the swelling leave my knees. I seemed to be enveloped in a white, billowing, rolling cloud. I was terrified and fought against the cloud but it covered me. Whether it was fear that made the water stream from me I don't know. But after this profound experience I felt great, with little pain. Since then I have progressed rapidly.'

Recalling some of the sensations while in trance at the sanctuary, Joan refers to a rippling feeling through her body, a 'feeling of great peace, floating away from life's trials and tribulations.' She feels tremendous, radiant heat from the healer's hands as she slips into trance. 'I feel very heavy, then weightless and drift off into space.' Since the treatments began Joan's weight has fallen dramatically from thirteen stone to nine stone. The healer also surprised her by diagnosing that she had a kidney complaint, a point she had never mentioned. That night she was violently sick.

'Cain warned me that this might happen. After the sickness my kidneys began functioning normally again. I have had no trouble in that area since.

'When I first went to him, I was on a high dosage of cortisone. Now it has been reduced to $3\frac{1}{2}$ milligrams. I am confident this can be reduced by a further milligram, which is a feat by itself.'

Joan has improved out of all recognition. She is far happier with herself and with life generally, thanks to Cain's remarkable healing.

Another testimony to the Cain phenomena, which no other healer appears able to duplicate, comes from Marjorie Smitham of Childer Crescent, Little Sutton, Wirral. Her life was a misery through persistently severe headaches and wracking pains in her shoulders.

On her second and third visits she received the now famous manipulating and heat treatment, though Cain's hands did not touch her. But what startled her even more was that Cain's healing extends to her own home! Hundreds of his patients have experienced this incredible phenomenon when Cain's spirit helpers continue their manipulative treatment after they have left the sanctuary.

'Yes, I have received healing sitting in a chair in my lounge,' Marjorie states firmly. 'I felt my head go from side to side very gently. As happened at Cain's place, manipulation treatment began and my head began to go round very slowly, then gather momentum. I felt that every muscle in my neck was being stretched to the utmost. I had a bad headache at the time. I was fine next day.

'The following day the treatment started again quite involuntarily. This time I received heat treatment to my neck and arm. This session lasted about an hour. I returned to his sanctuary and, after treatment to my spine, all these strange movements occurred. During the session it appears I had been doing the deaf-and-dumb sign language, with which I am not familiar, as well as the movements of an exotic Indian dance. I also felt strongly that I was playing a piano and conducting an orchestra.

'I received heat treatment to my arm, which was being thrown about all over the place. It was an eerie, though wonderfully uplifting, experience. Towards the end I realised, forcibly and without any question, that the spirit power had entered my body. My heart was beating like mad. I felt I wanted to stamp my feet and grind my teeth. I seemed so cross about something I could not explain. I could hear Cain asking, "Who are you friend?" It was a fantastic moment.'

On her last visit to the sanctuary Marjorie was dumbfounded when the healer asked whether she had any anxiety about her left breast.

'How could he possibly have known that I was very worried? My basset hound had jumped and bit my left breast as he tried to grab the mail from my hand. Cain was told psychically that he had to give healing to that part. When I told him I was indeed worried about the injury, he then gave healing.'

Cain tells of the occasion when the phenomena exploded into seeming violence. A sufferer, a huge man, was being treated. He lapsed into the comatose state and was soon throwing his arms about. Cain playfully sparred with him. Then the patient punched him full in the face. His great, balled fist struck Cain violently on the nose.

'That kind of blow would have felled an ox. I certainly went through all the motions. I was sent crashing into the sanctuary wall with a resounding thud. I could, and should, have been badly hurt.'

But amazingly, he neither felt the blow nor the resultant collision with the wall. And there was no mark on his face, though he explored it gingerly, thinking that his nose must surely be smashed. 'I should have been down and out, even seriously injured. But there was nothing. It's impossible to explain the mechanics of such a weird incident. How do you attempt to explain a supernormal mystery?'

CHAPTER 10

HE DOES THE IMPOSSIBLE

THE case of the ex-professional footballer is enthralling. Edmund Kilshaw, now 56, of Huyton, Liverpool, who is a science teacher at St Columbas Comprehensive School, Huyton, was transferred in 1949 from Bury FC to Sheffield Wednesday. He played 19 matches for Wednesday when a fierce tackle dislocated his left knee and ripped all the ligaments. His career was finished.

For the next 27 years Edmund was in constant, sometimes unbearable, pain. Each year his stance became more bowed. His injured leg, which is still dislocated, with the knee blown up like the football he used to kick with such skill, was riddled with osteo-arthritis. Edmund was used as the 'guinea pig' in this country for cortisone treatment. The last time he went to a specialist he was told he had the knee of a man of 90 and that it was finished. There was no medical hope of doing anything for it.

The unpalatable decision was made for him. There was no point in going to a doctor any more. There was no treatment. Fortunately, Edmund was no stranger to spirit healing. After the injury he had treatment from one in Sheffield. 'It helped tremendously. I had hopes of recovering and getting back into professional soccer. Sadly the healer passed on.'

Then recently he read a story about Cain in the *Liverpool Echo*. It jogged memories of his previous contact with spirit healing. He sought Cain.

'After the first treatment things happened which I couldn't explain,' says Edmund. 'For example, not being able to walk properly, yet being made to run.' He felt a powerful compunction to return to Hillsborough, Sheffield Wednesday's famous ground, 'and ran from one end to the other. I actually sprinted and never felt better. I was being willed to perform what should have been an impossible task. I had faith and confidence that nothing untoward would happen. My sprint covered some 120 yards, and this three days after my first treatment by Cain.'

Later he walked about half-a-mile to catch a bus to his school. It was a remarkable episode. Edmund explains the significance: 'Normally if I see a bus coming, and I am some distance from the stopping area, I can't do anything about it. But on this occasion I galloped like hell for the bus.

'Later going to a funeral I hit the kerb and slipped. That would have been sheer agony before I met Cain. I never felt a thing. It seems as though I am being protected through the healing. I know my knee will become progressively better.'

Edmund goes into deep trance when Cain treats him. Muscles in his thigh ripple as the mysterious manipulation technique operates.

After his first healing he went home and ran upstairs. His startled wife stammered, 'I thought you had a bad leg?'

Cain readily demonstrates to interested observers the unique healing given to sufferers in his sanctuary. With Megan Williamson, 52, of Ellesmere Port, he requested his guide, Carl, to 'completely relax this body and do the healing.'

Then Cain sat nonchalantly in a chair, arms akimbo, just watching. Immediately the frail Megan was having her head swivelled violently from side to side, a movement which normally she could not, and certainly would not, attempt. Her left leg raised itself from the floor in quick tempo. Her left shoulder rotated freely.

Deep in trance, her left leg movement increased considerably and her hips were manipulated, exercises that clearly would have been impossible for her to perform on her own.

Megan suffered a cerebral hemorrhage and thrombosis in 1968. It left her completely paralysed on the left side. She was in hospital for three months. She was able to walk only with a caliper.

'A friend had been to Cain. I decided that as doctors seemed to think I was no more than a cabbage that I would seek the healer's help. I am so glad I did. My friend's troublesome tennis elbow was completely cured. I am ecstatic over my improvement. My walking is marvellous. I have dispensed with the heavy iron caliper. My arm no longer pulls me to one side. It is now moving with me when I walk. I just don't bother with doctors and hospitals any more. Cain is my doctor now!

'Through him my life has changed dramatically. Now I can do my housework and shopping without difficulty. Before it was a continuous struggle. My left leg, which was rigid, now bends naturally as I walk. People remark on the difference in my gait since I came to Cain.

'When being treated I am aware what is going on. But when the manipulations begin I can't stop them. It feels as though someone is inside me pulling the strings.'

Irene Porter, 36, married with two children, of Ascot Drive, Bebington, Wirral, has been a laboratory technician for 20 years. But she has never seen anything in her lab to compare with the wonders of Cain's healing sanctuary.

Two years ago, overnight, she contracted rheumatoid arthritis in all her joints. She was left virtually crippled. The condition was not helped by a spell in hospital when traction treatment went wrong and a hip was taken out of joint.

Her visits to Cain have been startling. She went into trance and 'heard music. I thought I saw an old man in a gown touch me. He said I had to do exercises. He took hold of my leg and stretched it. I put my foot out. I could feel it tugging at my hip. This pulling seemed to go on for ages. The old man told me that when I felt the urge to exercise my leg to do exactly as he had done, to let my leg relax and it would then be manipulated.

'After that the leg straightened and I never had any more trouble with it. Before that my foot was bent and I could hardly walk. I couldn't take any pressure on my right leg.'

When Irene went into hospital in 1976 she couldn't even pick up a teaspoon. She was unable to feed herself. She was in constant 'screaming agony.'

After Cain's successful ministration, in which her pain miraculously vanished, she felt she could have 'leapt over his gate and bolted with joy through Eastham.' Because she didn't have pain after the first treatment she didn't return to the sanctuary. For seven weeks she was blissfully pain-free. Cain had advised her to continue the spirit healing.

'That was my mistake,' says Irene ruefully. 'The pain returned and I lost no time in getting back to that wonderful healing room. Now I am vastly improved all round.

'I couldn't wait to tell my hospital doctor what had happened. He was amazed. Sedimentation tests proved I was telling the truth. After I told them about the spirit healing, out of interest they ran new blood tests. The result showed the count was normal. They couldn't believe it. On the strength of it I was excused visits for six months. I will be able to show them an even greater improvement next time. I am sure they will faint in disbelief!'

If her doctors could see her treatment in Cain's sanctuary they would be even more incredulous.

Not a word is spoken, but she becomes entranced. Cain does not peer commandingly into her eyes. He sits passively by her side. Irene's right arm stretches. She mutters a low groan as she slips back on to a cushion. The manipulation begins. Her hand, which she could not clench, opens and closes freely. It is a perfectly natural, co-ordinated movement. To see it one could not believe there was anything wrong. Except that a few minutes before stepping into the sanctuary she had demonstrated her patent inability to close the stiffened hand.

In trance, and while the healing goes on, Irene is obviously in a state of ecstasy as she whispers, 'All the pain is going.'

To watch someone who has lived with stupendous pain suddenly gain instant relief, without administering drugs or other man-made poisons, is an incredible, uplifting experience. It's almost as though that higher, superior intelligence is exhorting, 'This is the way to do it.' Why don't we listen?

Irene speaks of seeing Cain's guide. Her hands felt as 'though they were in mud packs.' Her shoulder is encased in it, too. She talks of the guide's animals coming through the sanctuary, including an ox.

It seems she may have visited one of the spirit world's lower astral planes in her trance state. She becomes emotional as she refers to a person 'they call the Mad One. He has terrible head pains. He is sick.' The pain is apparently transferred to Irene. She moans, saying: 'Oh, there's such sorrow. I want to love everyone, but I can't.'

She becomes desperately cold in the 'dark tunnel' through which she is returned to her body. It is a remarkable commentary on what it must be like to visit a more unsavoury part of the Other Side.

On waking Irene remembers nothing of the traumatic experience. She thought she had had a nice sleep. She felt warm and lovely, in marked contrast to how she was describing her predicament a few seconds earlier.

She clenches her hands. 'It's fantastic! This never ceases to amaze me. I feel as though I have been stretched a mile.' She wriggles her feet. 'It's beautiful,' she sighs. Her face is wreathed in smiles. That's happiness.

CHAPTER 11

STRENGTH THROUGH HEALING

IF Elizabeth Heffy, 53, of Edgerton Park, Rock Ferry, Birkenhead, could have been granted a wish it would have been that she had known about Cain years earlier. For had that been possible she now knows she would have been rescued from needless years of intense pain.

She suffered from a thyroid gland for 23 years. For this condition she found Cain just in time. She had been worried about her hospital's decision to operate. Cain's treatment made it unnecessary.

Elizabeth was 'virtually crippled' with rheumatism throughout the body. Today, proudly and with feeling, she describes herself as a 'new woman.' Before discovering the healer, her nerves were shattered. 'I couldn't sleep. I was a total wreck. Then I heard about Cain through my daughter's friend.'

'The first time I didn't feel anything through the healing. But I felt strangely relaxed when I got home. This was quite an achievement in itself. I used to cry all the time because I was so depressed. But every time I saw Cain I became more improved. I have grown in confidence. I used to be afraid to go out. I was on drugs for 18 years, and they were doing nothing for me. I lived at the doctor's. I went every week without fail.

'Being treated by Cain has been a remarkable experience. He has given me a new lease of life. I can't stop talking to people about it. I could never repay him for what he has done.'

Elizabeth still cannot believe that the rheumatics, which had immobilised her for so long, have gone. 'I used to have to drag myself around. It was agony. Now I move perfectly well. When I was going through all the rigmarole with doctors and hospitals I never thought I would recover.'

Daughter Valerie, 25, tells how spirit healing brings happiness to others. 'When Mother was bad with her nerves and irritable, she upset everyone at home. You never knew how she would react to anything. She was weepy and argumentative. But from the moment she started seeing Cain she became incredibly calmer, a completely different person. This was a wonderfully new experience for the family.'

A colleague at Valerie's office was instrumental in transforming the Heffy family's fortunes. Through Cain's ministrations she made a 'complete recovery' from spinal curvature.

'She told me how well she felt,' recalls Valerie. 'I asked about Cain, then secured an appointment for Mother.' The resultant developments thrilled the whole family.

Valerie's father also benefited. He had a swollen leg vein and suffered from sinuses. 'He is now completely cured,' says Valerie.

She, too, sings his praises. 'I also was a sinus sufferer. It caused pressure behind the left eye. My eye-sight was affected. I had to wear heavily tinted glasses. After the third treatment I felt the sinus was relieved and my eyes began to focus normally. They have been perfect ever since. So the whole family has been cured.'

She still talks wonderingly about an incident involving her frail, just-over-six-stone mother while shopping in a market one day. 'We were at a stall when a man came up struggling with two heavy cotton bales. He threw them over the counter. One fell towards Mother. She merely stuck a hand out and stopped it. The man looked round saying: "My goodness! I expected to see at least a 20-stone man there." He couldn't believe that such a frail little thing could have produced such a feat of strength.'

'Obviously,' she quips, 'spirit healing makes you strong!'

Watching Elizabeth under treatment in the Cain sanctuary is intriguing. She slips into trance as Cain and his son, John Jnr, place hands near, but not on, her. Then her body begins to vibrate in the most amazingly vigorous way. This, says Cain, is to release her tensions. She arches her back and flails her arms frantically. She is like a gymnast going through a series of complicated, highly energetic and beautifully co-ordinated exercises.

The Cains then stand to one side observing her actions, seemingly taking no further part in the proceedings, though obviously their power is instrumental in creating the supernormal conditions under which the discarnate treatment comes.

Next comes a remarkable spectacle. Elizabeth, so frail and puny, rises from the couch on which she has been prostrate and engages Cain in a frenzied wrestling match, reminiscent of some of the judo contests described earlier. Their arms thresh like high-powered windmill blades. It requires a superhuman effort by Cain to return the patient to the couch, where again the action continues at a furious pace.

It seems impossible that such a small, light woman, who not long ago was crippled with rheumatism throughout her body, could exert such strength and speed of movement that it took all the strength of a burly ex-blacksmith, with his large iron-hard hands, to subdue her.

When she is brought from her deep trance, Elizabeth says she remembers nothing of the extraordinary incident. 'I just feel so relaxed!' After such punishing vigour, and the strenuous wrestling, one expects to find her breathing heavily and drenched in perspiration. But a hand placed on her back shows her to be breathing quite normally. Her body was certainly not over-heated.

Surely, then, one has to look beyond a normal explanation in attempting to understand what is taking place in the blue-walled sanctuary of John Cain, spirit healer?

CHAPTER 12

SHE 'FEELS LIKE BALLET DANCER'

THE mysterious Cain influence has brought untold happiness to Nancy Johnson, 57, and husband William, 65, of Stanley Lane, Eastham. Nancy, a champion swimmer in her youth, tells of her remarkable recovery from the agonising arthritis that had 'got me beat.'

For three years from January, 1973, the pain in her right hip and right ankle was excruciating, 'almost unbearable,' says Nancy. Despite the continuous agony and many tears she stopped using drugs. The slight relief was 'not worth the side effects.'

When matters were complicated by William being ill with 'flu and bronchitis, Nancy wondered how she could manage the frequent trips upstairs to tend him. For three days she could not sit, 'standing being the best position.' Finally, in sheer desperation she contacted Cain 'about whose healing powers we had heard and read.'

Nancy knew it would be impossible for her even to attempt to use their car, let alone drive it. She had to ask a friend who had a larger vehicle.

'My friend almost had to lift me in and out. As I went along Cain's driveway, she joked, "I want to see you run down this path!" After my first treatment this is exactly what I did. My friend could not believe it. I stood by the car, touched my toes several times, swung my right leg up and down and felt like a ballet dancer.

'My consultation with Cain lasted about an hour. I was fully dressed, which is wonderful for arthritic sufferers as dressing and undressing is sheer agony. I was not attached to any wires or electrical equipment, and apart from telling the healer where the pain was there was no talking. As he laid his hand on the affected parts, I experienced a burning sensation for a few seconds. After this I felt the most wonderful feeling of complete relaxation. I was quite conscious, but felt myself bending over as far as I could go with no pain anywhere. Even though I had heard of his healing powers, I just could not believe at first that this 'miracle' had happened to me.

'I came home and almost ran upstairs to my husband. He was amazed.'

After the healing, and not feeling pain, she was able to lift furniture and even climb up and down on a chair to put up Christmas decorations which before healing would have been impossible. 'This is the first time for years that I have been entirely free of pain.'

Before she saw Cain, Nancy felt 'doomed to the agonising life of an arthritic, a condition which does not improve with advancing years.' She had begun to feel old. Now she 'feels marvellous. I am sure the pain of this complaint cannot be exaggerated. I only wish that other chronic sufferers could be treated by Cain. We in this part of the country are indeed fortunate and blessed that we are able to visit him. It is a privilege for which I am truly grateful.'

Like Nancy, William has also suffered the agonies of this widespread complaint. His twinges began in the left shoulder blade in 1955. Ten years later the pain was worse and creeping into his neck. His doctor and specialists confirmed arthritis was setting in. He rejected the customary pills and drugs, preferring to put up with the pain. By 1975 the pain was moving down his left arm and to the left side of his face.

He appealed to Cain for help. The result? 'After just one visit the pain in my left shoulder completely disappeared, the arthritis in my neck is 90 per cent better, and the head and arm pains have subsided considerably. Moving my head either way was an effort, the noises sounding like someone walking on gravel. My cure is genuine. I wish Cain astonishing success.'

Nancy gives a graphic description of a public healing demonstration by Cain at the Civic Centre, Bromborough. She was 'amazed by the spectacle as patients in trance went through violent exercises. A stout woman sat in an upright chair. Suddenly her head began to revolve with great force. I thought she would break her neck. I had never seen anything like it. But she was fine. Later I was staggered to learn that she had had to wear a collar for arthritis. All those who participated in these strenuous exercises were not exhausted.'

After her own healing her husband's friend, a magistrate, visited them. Nancy took the opportunity of describing her remarkable treatment. With the magistrate was his wife and her sister.

The sister, coincidentally, had arthritis in the neck. She sat in a chair listening to the conversation about Cain's spirit healing.

'Suddenly,' Nancy recounts, 'without warning her neck began to swivel violently. She was unable to stop it. She went deathly white. The magistrate and the others in the room naturally became alarmed by this incredible spectacle.' Nancy did her best to explain that the remarkable manipulation must have been activated by proxy means because she had been describing Cain's powers.

'Next day the unwitting patient telephoned delightedly to say that her previously rigid neck was free!'

CHAPTER 13

SCEPTIC LOSES HEADACHES

NERVES caused Jean Dawson, 40, of Bolton Road East, New Ferry, Wirral, to have a major breakdown. For nine years she struggled for recovery. But despite electric and insulin treatments she seemed to make little progress.

Her lucky day came when her sister-in-law, a hospital sister, told her about an arthritic patient they had been unable to help who recovered completely at Cain's hands. 'I had tried everything else, so I went to Cain,' Jean says. 'After only his second treatment all my severe headaches just went. I was on six tablets a day. It was marvellous to be free of pain after so many years.'

Her verdict on spirit healing? 'Simply fantastic. I had always been sceptical about the stories I heard. But no longer!'

Most people who obtain benefit from unorthodox healing – though Spiritualists regard spirit healing as the most natural process of all – are only too delighted to share their good fortune with others. Such was the case with Jean when she found her neighbour, Mona Edward, suffering tremendous pain after a hiatus hernia operation.

'She had a swelling above her stomach and was terribly depressed because she had been so ill. I told her about Cain. I had his photograph and gave it to her to see whether anything registered. I can go into trance by just gazing at it. Mona had not been eating properly for a long time. Then she just looked at the photograph. She thought she had dozed off. Regaining her senses she said she felt hungry. It was the first time she had enjoyed food for many months.

'After she attached the photograph to a miniature statue the object moved several times without being touched by a human hand. She couldn't believe it.'

Mona was treated twice by Cain. Her swelling vanished and 'she feels marvellous,' says Jean. She tells of an absorbing incident involving Mona in Cain's lounge. Cain, who often asks guide Carl to play pranks with his unsuspecting patients, said, 'Carl, take off this woman's boots!'

Mona wore zip up, knee-high leather boots. 'She seemed to tremble all over. Then her feet started shaking and her boots slipped off. She was in trance and didn't really know what was happening. I could never believe it had I not seen it for myself. It defies description when you are trying to explain how a "dead" man can remove your boots.'

But Jean's is not the only evidence about the discarnate guide's penchant for practical jokes. Ethel Humphreys, 70, of The Rake, Bromborough, who first met Cain when she had successful healing four years ago, was shopping in her local supermarket one day when inexplicably she found herself rooted to the spot.

'It seemed an interminable time before I could free myself to move on. This happened to me twice in the same store. I am convinced that I was under the influence of Cain's guide. It might well be that I had to stay on the spot concerned to prevent an accident of some kind. I felt embarrassed at the time, but later I heard of similar occurrences.

'A woman had had healing. As she walked outside and was about to step from the kerb into the road she found she couldn't put her right foot down. It was suspended. Then she boarded her bus to go home and found herself pinned by an invisible force to her seat. Try as she might she couldn't move. She resigned herself to going on to the bus terminal and then travelling back, but then found herself released just in time to alight at her stop. It seems Carl has a great sense of humour!'

Ethel, a proud member of Cain's physical home circle, has had her shoes removed several times at these meetings. 'Suddenly my foot is shaken and my shoe lands several feet away from the circle leader. We have experimented by trying to kick off my shoe in the same way, but it couldn't be done.'

Ethel was cured of arthritis in hips and knees. She had seen a report about Cain's work in *Birkenhead News*. Impressed, she contacted him and had several treatments. Her pains disappeared quickly and have never returned. She had previously been prescribed drugs by her doctor which made her ill.

She was already convinced of spirit healing's reality before she met Cain. Later she became a close friend to his mother, Nellie, 65.

Ethel has taken a personal interest in Cain's activities. 'He has a deep compassion for humanity. Basically he is a very kind person. He is not religious. But he believes there is a God. But he is not pious, nor is he demonstrative. He feels for people who need help. He is convinced this is what he is meant to do with his life. His beginning as a full-time healer was a difficult struggle after giving up his successful business.

'The trance stage in patients had only just begun when I went to him. We were all so interested in the things that were happening. I have been able to see the changes in his healing techniques. Two years ago I saw this black emanation extending from his arm to the patient. I told Cain what I saw.'

When she accompanied Cain to Stansted Hall, Ronald Baker, then the SNU general secretary, was asked for an explanation of the phenomenon. He said it was a type of energy power that was rarely visible to the naked eye. But since then, Ethel claims other patients have reported seeing the emanation.

Famous medium Ursula Roberts of Sunny Gardens Road, Hendon, NW London, told Ethel that 'undoubtedly Cain is developing new forms of healing.' She asked her guides to explain the unusual ray Ethel saw stretching along the healer's arm.

'They said the colour is not really black but is indigo, which sometimes can appear to be so dark that it is almost black. This colour ray is sometimes associated with a slight degree of ectoplasmic force which can be grey and light or dark in its colour. Undoubtedly, this extrusion of force from the medium through to the patients is that which is bringing about the unusual type of healing.'

Ethel has seen many dramatic instances of cures over the past four years. Once she noticed that a man had to stand against the wall because his condition would not allow him to sit without great discomfort. He came out of the sanctuary after his first healing, sat down . . . and was astounded by his action.

'I have seen so much, apart from my own experience, that there can be no possible doubt about Cain's remarkable ability to heal. He has achieved a really staggering success rate with arthritic cases. The remarkable thing is that, having had contact healing, invariably they report these mysterious manipulations taking place in their own homes, with many people going into trance.'

Once Ethel had a swollen finger and couldn't wear a ring. After Cain treated it, something roused her at 2 a.m. She lay in bed watching her hand and wrist being manipulated.

'It was clearly an external force at work. It is extraordinary.'

CHAPTER 14

JAPANESE FETE HIM

CAIN is a 'pin-up-boy' to hundreds of Oriental women. He received a surprise invitation to make his first visit to Japan in the summer of 1976. Two weeks before his Tokyo invitation arrived by post, the healer remarked to his home circle that he would like to visit Japan. He has always felt a strong affinity with that country. One of his guides is Japanese.

He spent a week as guest of the Shogakukan Publishing Company, Tokyo. A programme was arranged by its 600,000-circulation women's weekly magazine, 'Josei Seven'. Cain treated about 60 sufferers for a special in-depth article. The patients were selected by the magazine.

A preliminary story about Cain had the magazine's switchboard swamped with callers. His treatment sessions were held in the editorial offices. Three reporters and a team of photographers were commissioned to cover the programme.

Observers were surprised when Cain brought a young Japanese woman's latent psychic gifts to the surface. Her automatic writing in English was done 'at fantastic speed.'

Masahiro Masui, the assistant editor of 'Josei Seven,' called Cain's demonstration 'magnificent. We received more than a thousand letters from readers requesting your photograph. We sent one to all.'

The Japanese-compiled report of Cain's outstandingly successful demonstration, involving 23 patients selected from a thousand of the magazine's readers, describes how the Japanese responded to his healing.

A chronic rhinitis sufferer, Suzuko Hiraki, 30, became entranced after Cain touched her. Emiko Yoshida, a 32-year-old office girl, was treated for rheumatism. She 'felt heat and my body leant backward as if pulled by some invisible force.'

Cain treated a three-year-old boy with paralysis, Kenichi Isozaki. The boy's response to his healing touch is described as 'wonderful. As Cain moves his hand above him, Kenichi's hands and legs move in unison.' He went into trance for 20 minutes.

Later a special check was made on the boy's condition. Delightedly his mother reported that Kenichi had fed himself for the first time, using his paralysed right hand. Before seeing Cain she had to feed him by spoon.

At the demonstration Cain used 'Josei Seven's' editor-in-chief, Mamoru Okada, to heal diabetes sufferer Kyoko Hori, 26.

'The result was fantastic,' adds the report. 'Okada manages to put Miss Hori into trance in five minutes.' Later she said she felt heat when Okada placed hands over her head, adding, 'I feel wonderful.'

The Japanese observers were astonished by the next incident. Mrs Sayoko Masuda, suffering with a nasal allergy, watched Cain's picture while waiting for the healer. From the other side of the room Cain merely waved his hand, as though giving a silent instruction. Sayoko suddenly slipped into trance, falling back on a bed.

'The way this happens is truly amazing,' says the report.

Next came 30-year-old housewife Yoshiko Sasamoto, who could walk only with crutches. A severe rheumatics case since December,

1974, she fell into trance immediately Cain's hands passed over her head. On recovering she announced, 'I feel fine.' But far more drama was to follow. As she began to move back to her seat among the audience, her husband handed her a pair of crutches. But Cain whisked them away, ordering the surprised woman to walk by herself. She did so.

'She stops and looks back at Cain as if she cannot believe what she is doing,' says the report. Cain smiles, asking how she feels. With a shy smile she replies, "Great. And there is no pain at all!" Cain encouraged her telling her that she could walk without crutches. It is the first time since she became ill that she has been able to walk unaided. This spectacular happening brings spontaneous, frenzied applause from the wide-eyed audience. The drama of a crippled woman walking touches their hearts. Suddenly Cain's name is on everybody's lips.'

Cain had worked seven hours without a break, fortified only by the occasional nip of whisky.

Later, says the report, Cain cut short a sightseeing tour to Kyoto to treat a 10-year-old Japanese boy with muscular dystrophy.

'Within ten seconds the boy went into trance and responded violently to Cain's touch. He moved his paralysed legs. Shortly he fell from the bed because he moved too vigorously. Cain stood away from the bed and made various movements with his body. The entranced boy, eyes closed, performed exactly the same moves. He could not possibly have seen what Cain was doing. For example, when the healer patted his chest with his fist, the boy copied him. Normally the boy would merely sit motionless in his wheelchair. He emerged from his 90-minute trance saying he felt terrific and still seemed to be moving.'

The thorough, ultra-professional Japanese checked on Cain before inviting him to visit them. Toshiya Nakaoka, a psychic researcher and noted author on paranormal subjects in Japan, tested Cain in London. Later he despatched a 'highly impressed' communiqué to his colleagues in Tokyo.

Nakaoka's test was a telepathic one involving two patients. Cain was asked to bring a recumbent patient into a sitting position, make her open her eyes and look around the room. The other one was to be brought to a sitting position from a comatose state at precisely 3 p.m. Nakaoka was delighted when Cain accomplished the feats.

But he was even more astonished when a Japanese woman colleague noting the proceedings suddenly slipped into trance!

It was no surprise when, only five months after his first highly-successful trip, Cain was invited by Nakaoka to return. This time the mission was to see whether spirit power could save a desperately ill man from a major operation.

The man, Mr Sonoda, whom Cain did not know and had never met, was suffering from a number of serious complaints, including partial paralysis in arms and legs and a damaged spine.

A report says Sonoda responded encouragingly to the healing. Some of his pain was greatly relieved. Previously his gait was like that of a drunken man, but after the healing he walked straight. The planned operation on his spine was averted for the time being due to Cain's intervention. Sonoda was so heartened by the improvements effected in his condition that he planned to visit Cain in England for further treatment.

During this second visit to Tokyo, Cain underwent scientific tests conducted by Dr Niroshi Motoyama, Director of the Japanese Institute for Religious Psychology and president of the International Association for Religious Parapsychology.

CHAPTER 15

CANADIANS SALUTE HIS POWER

IN September, 1976, Cain, ever willing to demonstrate his powers for which he claims no credit, discovered his fame had spread to North America. He was asked to stage healing demonstrations. His sponsor was Vancouver businessman Charles Mitchell who had earlier sought Cain's absent healing for his serious illness. He was so impressed with his general improvement that he beseeched Cain to fly to Canada to give him contact healing.

Cain had warned there was not much chance because of the advanced state of his illness. Mitchell implored him to do what he could. He had nothing to lose because medicos could do nothing more.

Mitchell telephoned his SOS to Cain. And he is certain that

his transatlantic call activated the spirit healing process. For in the early hours following his call he was awakened. It seemed as though he had been pushed by someone. But there was no one else in his room. To his astonishment, he found that he had no more pain.

After Cain gave him contact healing, within a few weeks Mitchell reported that he had put on 11 lbs in weight. Both in Vancouver and Winnipeg, 1,800 miles away, Cain held group healings. Dozens of people delightedly reported they had been helped by the healer's power.

But Cain's most outstanding result was with muscular dystrophy sufferer, Donna Hills of Knight Road, Vancouver. It seemed impossible that anything could be done to help her sad condition. Her back was four inches out of alignment and her stomach extended like a pregnant woman.

Immediately Cain placed hands on her she went into trance when her legs and spine were manipulated and 'stretched.' The swollen stomach receded. In order to walk Donna had to hurl her arms about vigorously to aid her propulsion. But after Cain's fourth treatment she began walking normally, except for a single arm movement.

After Cain returned to his Wirral home he had a letter from Donna. It makes remarkable reading:

'Just after you left, I hadn't found any more improvements. Then, a week ago, I was cold for three days. (It will be recalled that an earlier patient described being in a frozen state after the healer treated her). I couldn't get warm. After that I had a bad headache for two days, also a terrible backache. Next I felt pulling in my legs. Occasionally at three o'clock in the morning I wake up and feel as though I am floating. This has happened four times since you left.

'Last week I had another great experience. I walked about one-and-a-half blocks without even feeling tired. Before I would have had to stop and rest for a minute. I just couldn't believe it.'

Another Canadian also sings the praises of Cain's spirit healing. Albert Williams of Bates Road, Richmond, British Columbia reports what happened after his father, Jack, was treated by Cain for a severe chest complaint which had made him so incapacitated he had to retire from work ten years earlier.

'The improvement in his chest condition,' says Williams, 'can only be described as fantastic. Very much against my wishes, he went swimming four or five times. That is amazing when one knows that he has not done so for over 20 years. He was also kicking a football and running with my sons on many occasions, without any ill-effects.

'We were delighted to hear him whistling and singing. Only a couple of months earlier he could hardly breathe.'

Williams told Cain: 'Whatever the power you have directed at my Dad has helped him immensely. All his family will be forever grateful.'

This kind of tribute is commonplace. Cain's files bulge with testimonials from people all over the country, and many parts of the world, who have benefited from his spiritual powers.

Arthur King of Starbeck Drive, Little Sutton, Wirral, wrote to his local paper, *Ellesmere Port Pioneer,* after an article on Cain's healing. He tells how the healer brought relief in one treatment to his wife that 120 mgs of morphine per day could not.

'When we saw Cain for the first time we didn't ask for a cure. We asked for one good night's sleep. He did this. Now she is sleeping better, eating better and feeling better. If Cain had told me to throw my wife out of the window and she would get relief, I would have done just that. I have no doubt in my mind that Cain has done a wonderful job on my wife. I don't need a logical explanation. The woman I married is still here with me. If she had stayed on that amount of morphine for much longer, most likely she would have been in the cemetery.

'If these scientists had suffered the pain my wife has, logic would not come into it. Once again I will say that Cain never said he would cure my wife, but he would bring her relief from pain. He did say that if she was cured it would be from a far greater power than his. My wife is suffering from a malignant cancer.'

People in all walks of life, professional and non-professional, happily testify to what they see and hear when they or acquaintances come into Cain's magnetic orbit.

One such is D. H. English, a senior engineer at a famous Ellesmere Port motor manufacturing plant. He also told the *Pioneer* about the man he calls 'the remarkable healer at Eastham.' What he knew 'for absolute certain is that John Cain has access to a definite unseen healing power, which so far, has given positive relief to at least 80 per cent of patients visiting his healing sanctuary in Rothesay Drive.'

English was eventually able to persuade two of his business associates, both under orthodox medical treatment, to spare but an hour of their leisure time to test for themselves the result of a Cain session.

'Both men were, as expected, extremely sceptical. Both worked on the same staff as myself, thus affording me opportunity to observe any noticeable improvement following healing sessions. My friend living at Whitby had been forced to take pain-killing drugs for nine months, suffering extreme pain in the legs and spine which had been diagnosed as sciatica, disc trouble or strained back.

'The first visit to Cain was disappointing. Nothing appeared to improve. Luckily my colleague, sceptic though he was, decided to continue with a weekly visit. After four visits he was able to go days without taking pain-killer pills and sleeps and walks better; so much so, that foremen on the shop floor have remarked how well he looks.

'My other colleague, also living in the Borough, was knocked off his bicycle by a car some months ago and suffered damage to his left arm. Weeks of conventional treatment and exercises still left him with much pain and many sleepless nights. He was a sceptic, too. Never heard of spiritual healing, but wisely decided to "have a go – it couldn't get much worse; it might get better?" After only three visits to Cain he was signed off by a consultant specialist from a local hospital, and by his own doctor. Neither knew why nor what was responsible for his speedy recovery.'

Exhorting sufferers to seek spirit healing, English concludes: 'If your doctor has said, "Sorry, you've got to learn to live with it!" perhaps you might. But there's always a possibility you needn't.'

CHAPTER 16

SHE DANCED ALL NIGHT!

ELECTRICAL engineer Ray Cumin, 49, of Longdale Drive, Chester, met Cain in 1972 when the healer was being hailed as an exciting new discovery. Cumin was intrigued. He was certainly no stranger to spirit healing. His mother was treated successfully by Harry Edwards many years before.

He decided he would test the newcomer's powers. He took a woman suffering with severe arthritis. She couldn't stand. It took her an hour to leave her bed.

Says Cumin: 'The first time there was a great improvement. The second time the improvement was so dramatic she went out dancing all night! By the third healing she was completely cured. I was impressed, but not surprised because I expected a result. I accepted the phenomena. The woman concerned returned to full-time work and has never looked back. She had been stricken with arthritis for ten years.'

Next Cumin wondered whether Cain could help his son, Anthony, then 12, who had an unsightly birthmark on his left side. He was extremely self-conscious of it. On the first healing it shrank significantly in size, though Cain himself did not believe anything would happen. Later the skin texture changed to a golden hue. Today it looks just like an ordinary mole.

One day Cumin was shocked to see Malcolm Bowes, then 12, of Chester, in a wheelchair. He was an advanced muscular dystrophy victim. His father had built the Cumin's home. Cumin told the boy's cousin about Cain. It led to Malcolm being treated at the sanctuary.

Says Cumin: 'After two or three visits the boy began to sit upright in his chair, which he had not been able to do. Then, amazingly, on his matchstick legs calf muscles developed. An operation-type scar appeared on his left groin, which flabbergasted everybody. Malcolm described how he could feel fingers moving inside him. His crooked hips began to straighten. He is greatly improved. He has been given at least another five years' life which I am sure he would not otherwise have had.'

At that time Cain had two helpers, Glyn Holmes and Ronnie Dennis. For some reason Ronnie was absent one afternoon and Glyn had a row with his wife about his spending so much time at the sanctuary.

Cain nodded toward Cumin, 'You are working this afternoon!' After that, strangely, neither Ronnie nor Glyn came back. Cumin had never done any healing before. It was a year before he realised he was not just acting as a helper, but was healing in his own right.

He helped Cain with a terminal cancer patient. The disease was relieved. She passed on a year later – through a stroke! An autopsy revealed no trace of cancer.

Cumin is certain his partnership with Cain is planned by the Other Side. He expresses great admiration for his healer-in-chief, of whom he says, 'So far as I am concerned, his healing phenomena are unique.'

He talks of the 'supernormal power released here' being so intense that it 'would frighten ordinary doctors to death! In fact, there is nothing to be alarmed about. It is all controlled by this higher intelligence, and you know nothing wrong can happen. It is all directed to the human good.'

Cumin is 'fully prepared' to give up his business life to join Cain in his crusade. 'I shall be more than happy when that day comes.'

He says the percentage success rate of cures and improvements effected in healing sessions at the sanctuary is between 80-85 per cent.

One of these statistics is former hospital nurse Myra Heatley of Bebington. Spinal arthritis ended her career. In desperation she went to Cain early in 1977.

'I had been in continuous pain day and night. It was getting me down. Each session with Cain brought an improvement.'

Once she had to spend most of the day in bed. But now she is 'great. I never expected to get this kind of improvement so quickly. It is my first experience of spirit healing. My verdict? It's marvellous! I am now completely free of pain.'

Then there is the case of Gwen Snow, 62, of Terminus Road, Bromborough, who was the centrepiece of poltergeist phenomena after being treated by Cain.

Over the past ten years she had had two thyroid operations. Another lump appeared in the front of her neck near the last one that had been removed. Worried by the awful choking sensation, she went back to her local hospital only to learn that the new condition was inoperable.

She happened to read about Cain in a paper. She made an appointment.

'After a few visits the lump vanished. There was no more discomfort. It is fantastic. Then I experienced this eerie poltergeist phenomena which I can only attribute to Cain's influence.'

Gwen was in her kitchen by the end wall unit. 'I got this awful feeling like a cold breeze blowing. I raised my arm to open the cupboard door when the unit came down. It laid on my arm which was absolutely stretched. Eggs and tins were falling around me. I had the unit's full weight on my arm. My husband shouted to me to let it go. But I couldn't. My arm was solid. Amazingly nothing was broken. Eggs, jars of jam and pickles fell to the floor from a height of about six feet. Everything was intact. I just didn't feel the tins and jars as they hit my head on their way down. When my husband took the weight from my arm I walked away.'

Another incident in the kitchen happened the day she had visited Cain for further treatment. She went to the sink to do something.

'I felt as though I had gone as stiff as a board. It was uncanny. I shouted to my husband that I couldn't move. He pulled at me. I didn't budge. I was completely locked to the spot. I felt that some power was holding me.'

Later she went to the 'fridge and something stopped her in her tracks. 'I experienced this strange cold breeze again.'

Husband Harry confirms the details of his wife's experiences in the ghost-plagued kitchen. Of the falling wall unit he says: 'It would have had to be some considerable force to get the cabinet away from the wall because it was newly fixed with three-inch rawlplugs and screws. I was amazed by the spectacle when my wife called me. Her arm felt like a solid bar.'

CHAPTER 17

TESTIMONIALS GALORE

Cain, as with all Spiritualist healers, discounts the term 'faith healing.' After all, they reason, you can't expect children or animals to have faith that they will be made well. Yet the annals of spirit healing show countless cases of such healing. So it is clear that faith is not a necessary adjunct to the process; it is not a pre-requisite to successful healing. Thus there are many illustrations of sceptics and agnostics getting remarkable results.

It is always more gratifying to Cain when a sceptic, someone who perhaps disbelieves in the phenomena to such an extent that he comes to scoff, receives undeniable healing benefit. His impressive list of testimonials include many acknowledgements from people who came to him as a last resort but not thinking they could really be helped.

One such is Winifred Baines of Dunster Grove, Gayton Heswall, Wirral, who received a complicated compound leg fracture after a road accident in 1959. Her letter reads: 'Today I have had some healing from your miracle hands. I was sceptical when I first came. I thought, "Well, if you don't do me any good, you couldn't possibly make me feel worse.' My right leg was in a very poor condition, badly swollen and discoloured almost to the knee. I didn't know what it was like to be without pain. I was afraid to approach my doctor as I thought he would say "Hospital!" Every time I lifted my feet it was agony. They just felt raw. My movements were very restricted.

'If I said I had ten minutes' pain since my healing first started, I would be telling an untruth. It is quite embarrassing. People now stop me wanting to know what has happened! A nursing sister, who is interested, told me I looked ten years younger. Strange, I feel 20 years younger, despite my 73 years. My family and I will always be grateful to you for giving me back my health.'

Madge Wilkinson of Frogmore Road, Blackwater, Camberley, Surrey, suffered back agony for 25 years before finding instant cure from Cain's ever-willing hands. She writes: 'I developed a pain in my right side. I went to hospital for X-rays and was told I had a trapped nerve in my side. I had no treatment, only a steel corset which I could not wear. I then went to Reading, Berkshire, to a private spine specialist and had more X-rays. I had treatment twice a week for nearly two years. Then he told me he could do nothing more. He asked me to go to another doctor at Banbury. I took the X-rays with me. He told me my back was in a terrible state, which I already knew. He suggested I go to Oxford to have another steel corset made. I did, but still could not wear it. We went to Stansted, Essex, for a holiday and attended your healing demonstration. Tom (her husband) asked if you would give me healing. You said you would in the evening with several other people.

'I was a bit worried at the time, but thought I would try anything. I believe I was out (comatose state) for $1\frac{1}{2}$ hours. It felt as though my right leg was in a concrete block, getting shorter all the time. It felt as though an electric current was going through my body, and something heavy was pressing on my head. Then I felt a click in my back. Though I could not move, I could hear voices in the distance. Eventually I recovered my senses. You and your friend helped me to walk across the room. I had no pain. Lumps which I had on my fingers, and one on the front of my leg caused by a kick from a horse, had disappeared. I could have cried with joy. I tell all our friends about your wonderful work and the cures you had at Stansted. I believe there were eight.

'We have now moved to a bungalow with a third-of-an-acre allowing plenty of gardening. I have a part-time job in a greengrocer's shop. I can bend and lift with no pain at all.'

Margaret Dunn of Dawpool Drive, Bromborough, Wirral, tells what happened when her son, Kevin, was born toward the end of 1973. 'He was premature and weighed only 4 lb. 1 oz. At four weeks they found he had a heart murmur. X-rays showed one side of the heart enlarged. Cardiograph readings revealed the heart was not perfect.

'The heart specialist from Liverpool told us Kevin had a hole in the heart and would need surgery later. I contacted John Cain and went to him regularly with Kevin. He was a blue baby and puny, but as the months went by he progressed very well. At 20 months he went into hospital for more X-rays and tests. Tubes were put through his leg artery to the heart. Results were very pleasing as the doctors could not find what they had previously diagnosed. X-rays showed Kevin's heart was back to normal shape. The doctors were amazed. They had told us not to expect a miracle. To us that miracle happened once we started our visits to Mr Cain. Now Kevin is of normal height and weight for a three-year-old. Mr Cain will always be remembered for what he has done for us.'

Ruth Butterwood of Kings Lane, Bebington, Wirral, writes: 'My brother suffered for years from the distressing effects of an allergy caused by leaf dust and asthma throughout his Service life in the R.A.F., the medical profession being able to relieve the attacks only by using drugs. During one very severe attack, and in desperation, he went to John Cain. After one visit all the miseries of his complaint had gone and a year has now passed without any recurrence.

'After seeing the amazing effects and results of his healing, I then asked John to help my sister who in early 1970 suffered a severe right-sided stroke which left her with a limp in her right leg, no use in her right arm and hand, plus impaired speech, which made communication difficult. Before attending John, my sister had for a period of more than four years had hospital therapeutic treatment with no visible signs of improvement in her condition. From her first visit to John, both my husband and myself were amazed at the outcome.

'While in a state of trance, and with no physical contact with John, my sister started moving both her right arm and leg. Now, after further treatment, she is 95 per cent normal in using these limbs and in her speech. She has since been medically examined and passed fit to again drive a car.

'In February, 1976, my husband was involved in a serious car accident. Although wearing his seat belt, he suffered extensive internal bruising and great pain in his right shoulder due to the force of impact. He decided to contact John, with the result that after one treatment and three days of absent healing the shoulder pain, which prevented arm movement, was completely cured.'

Elwyn Prichard-Jones of Glan Rhyd Estate, Dinas, Caernarvon, North Wales, writes: 'Following our conversation on the telephone last night, I returned to the house to sit quietly with my wife, Rhiannon, for 45 minutes. As soon as we sat, with your photograph on my wife's knee, we began to get a faint, but definite, sensation of pressure . . . our hair 'creeping' and something like a light but indefinable pressure on our temples and elsewhere around the head. Each night as we sit like this, Rhiannon seems to go to sleep for a minute or two, suddenly waking with a slight ticklish cough, which we imagine is due to the healing going on in the thyroid gland.

'As I said on the telephone, we are extremely excited by the indisputable change in my wife's appearance. There is a great increase in her capacity to do the house work without complaining of terrible fatigue. The disfiguring puffiness of her face, and the swelling of her nose, has been reduced considerably. Her almost continuous trembling has virtually ceased. Many people have commented on her cheerfulness. Unquestionably you are reaching us. This is extremely encouraging, for she has been ill for about 16 years. She has been treated previously by doctors, homeopathic practitioners, healers both famous and less well-known, without the slightest effect. It is a great and wonderful change for me to hear my dear wife say she has no pain in her thyroid gland. Somehow I feel that a complete cure will be effected. Regarding myself, my left middle ear condition is very much improved today.'

These testimonials are but a random sample of hundreds in Cain's possession. But they serve to illustrate that, but for the ex-blacksmith and his healing hands, many sufferers who found their way to his sanctuary might still be living in wretched, pain-filled misery today.

PART II
by
JOHN CAIN

PART TWO

CHAPTER ONE

SINCE the publication of *HEAL, MY SON! – the amazing story of John Cain* – by Peter Green, eight years have passed. For the last four years the book has been out of print, but the demand has been such that I take this opportunity of describing the development of my healing work and other aims I have realised since.

The developments since 1977 have been sometimes slow, sometimes very rapid, but there has been a natural evolution towards a more 'gentle' method.

Because of the ever-increasing demand for healing I was forced to work excessivley long hours and that alone was very difficult to sustain. It became apparent some time later that I had to pay a heavy price for those long hours.

It was during this period that my son, John Cain Junior came to the forefront and began sharing the heavy work-load with me, and it soon became apparent that he too had an extraordinary ability to heal and is, indeed, able to conduct healing sessions as well as myself.

When I subsequently suffered a heart attack in 1983 it was John Cain Junior who took over the entire healing work and he has continued to serve the hundreds of patients who come for healing; since 1983 he has worked as a healer on a full-time basis.

At the John Cain Healing Centre in Birkenhead, my son John Cain Junior is bearing most of the burden of healing, ably assisted by my wife Audrey and Ethel Humphreys and helpers like Stella and Donald Prescott, who travel 500 miles a week to serve the sick.

I am particularly happy that my son John has progressed both

John Cain and his son John Cain Junior, who has followed in his father's footsteps. Today John Cain Junior bears most of the burden of healing at the Healing Centre in Birkenhead.

as a healer and a medium through whom the 'Life Force' can work beyond all expectations. I cannot pay tribute enough to John both as a person and as a healer, and I am proud as his father that he has earned the highest respect and admiration from all the patients who have been treated by him.

From 1977 onwards until the present time, and I expect it will continue, I became more and more aware of two parrallel and corresponding developments: my own personal development and spiritual awareness and that of the healing itself. Remarkably these developments could also be seen to take place in my son John and his work as well as in the helpers who assist us in our work.

Perhaps this is the right moment to refer the reader to two other publications: the *JOHN CAIN HEALING GUIDE* by Valerie Wooding, which, as the title suggests, introduces the newcomer to some of my methods and also the responses from the patient; and also *YOU DON'T KNOW JOHN CAIN?* by Pat Sykes and introduced by Alan Whittaker, the senior feature writer of the *News of the World*. The latter is a comprehensive list of case histories with additional contributions by notable scientists such as Dr. Malcolm Hughes, M.Sc., (London), B.Sc., (Hons., London).

There is no doubt that much that has been written about the esoteric in general, and healing in particular, has been written and reviewed in the press and media with great scepticism, apathy and, sometimes, total rejection and hostility.

I, as a private person, and my healing have been frequently subjected to investigations by the press and the media. I have always, without exception, agreed to any reasonable request for interviews and experiments and in most cases, often after an hour or two, the journalists and their experts who usually accompanied them told me quite frankly that the editor had sent them on the assignment to 'expose' a charlatan or some half-wit or even religious maniac. Every investigating journalist carried out his enquiry according to his own methods, and I have never attempted to influence what they were doing. Some admitted to preconceived ideas and even prejudices, and on more than one occasion journalists told me that scandal or exposure of fraudulent methods sold more copies than a straight forward report of a successful healing.

Perhaps some examples will better illustrate my relationship with the press and the media than general comments could.

Kieran Devaney of Radio City Liverpool presented two major programmes called "Beyond Belief". In the summer of 1984 Radic City intended to do a major exposé on me. Although a local radio station, it caters for the entire area of Merseyside and beyond.

I have both programmes on tape and because they were rather long programmes I restrict myself to extracting just some of the sentences of the commentator and some of the patients interviewed.

" . . . and here at Bromborough Civic Hall between 50 and 60 people wait expectantly; some are on crutches, some are carried, some are lying on beds unable to walk and there are also some here just out of curiosity. But they have all come here to see and meet one man: his name is John Cain. . .

"Cain himself refuses to talk about cures but he

acknowledges the fact that he has extraordinary powers. . .

"with John Cain's agreement we have decided on a series of unusual scientific tests; tests which will start with a machine capable of probing the depth of John Cain's brain activity. . .

" . . . and with me is Ted Simpson, a Psychotherapist who has his practice in Liverpool's Rodney Street, the 'Harley Street' of the North. The machines John Cain is being wired to are called 'Mind Mirrors'. Ted Simpson first connects Elaine Vickers to a Mind Mirror and then John Cain to a separate one.

"As Ted Simpson monitors the instrument he notices something rather unusual . . . when we started this experiment Elaine's and John's Mind Mirrors showed totally different readings as one would expect from different individuals with different likes and dislikes and different reactions; but suddenly they are showing both the same basic metabolic rate.

"This suggests that whatever is going on in John's mind, whatever is happening there, somehow there appears to be a corresponding and matching activity in Elaine's nervous system . . . there is a very rapid beta activity; it definitely looks from here as though she is wide awake and yet at the same time she is producing the kind of waves which the normal person produces on the verge of very deep sleep. Both brain patterns are now the same on the monitors."

Ted Simpson the Psychotherapist had admitted to being very sceptical of John Cain's claims when the investigation and the experiments started. By the end of the second afternoon of experiments he had clearly changed his mind:

"What is your reaction to this series of experiments so far?" Trying to be objective about it, I think astonishment is the word. It appears as if the patient's mind follows that of John Cain. And yet, with the knowledge we have at present it is difficult to understand why that should be so. It has to be seen to believed, and on the face of it it's incredible."

Ted Simpson's experiments proved that incredible changes took place both in my brain and that of my patient Elaine Vickers, during the healing sessions. I have lost count of the number of times I have offered myself to the medical profession for tests and experiments but the verdict has always been the same according to the press "John Cain remains beyond belief". Simpson's programmes lasted half an hour each.

I remember the magazine *Reveille* carrying out an experiment. My publishers in Gerrards Cross had been approached by the magazine's editor who later became a director of the *Mirror Group* of newspapers, with the request that he be allowed to send his most sceptical journalist to investigate John Cain. He had called the book *HEAL, MY SON!* too good to be true. Also he made the condition that the journalist would turn up unannounced and anywhere I might be giving healing.

My publishers had also agreed not to tell me about this forthcoming 'investigation' and the journalist would not identify himself as such unless he would choose to do so. If he were to identify himself I was to telephone my publishers who would ask me to give the person my full co-operation.

As it happened no journalist from *Reveille* ever identified himself, but he obviously came with his wife and mother-in-law as 'ordinary patients to my Healing Centre'.

To everybody's amazement the *Reveille* issue of the 9th September 1977 carried as its main feature a large article with the banner headline: **"AMAZING!" – That's my verdict on healer John Cain, says Reveille writer** –

"I was walking up this mountain road when I met my father-in-law. We stopped and talked for a while. My uncle and grandfather were with him, but they didn't say anything.

This happened only the other day . . . yet my grandfather died in 1961, my uncle in 1972 and my father-in-law two years ago.

I was in what blacksmith-turned-spirit-healer John Cain calls an "altered state of consciousness" when the strange encounter took place.

In the back room of his bungalow at Eastham, Cheshire, John had put me "under" as he worked on my back trouble.

No staring eyes or incantations. You just let yourself go because you feel that's what John wants you to do.

Eyes shut, I lay relaxed on a couch.

I was completely aware of John's hands moving about my body and I could hear him talking to my wife and mother-in-law, who were in the room with us.

At the same time, though, I was conscious of being away from things.

I was aware that I stopped breathing several times for what seemed like ages. John explained later that this was because in such a relaxed state my body needed less oxygen.

Heat seemed to radiate intensely from John's palms. Then I saw flashes of white light in front of my eyes—and suddenly I was on that mountain road, talking to my dead father-in-law.

I didn't actually hear him speak. It was as if his words were being planted in my head.

Similarly, I seemed to be able to talk to him without speaking.

"Why don't you come over?" he asked.

"I'm not ready yet", I told him. "Give me another 50 years!"

The three of them—my father-in-law, grandfather and uncle—seemed disappointed.

They went away; and I carried on up the mountain.

I was relieved later when John Cain told me I wasn't being invited over for good!

"They wanted you to have an out-of-the-body experience and see what life is like in the spirit world", he told me. "Healing seems to stimulate the psychic glands and a lot of my patients have terrific out-of-the-body experiences. "They get among the crowds who've gone over and I hear them laughing and chatting away to parents and people they haven't seen since childhood".

All the time I had also been aware that I was lying on a couch in John Cain's bungalow.

As the vision faded, I heard John telling my wife and mother-in-law how some of his patients had conversations with loved ones who had passed away.

Not wishing to cause my mother-in-law any distress. I didn't say anything about my "vision" at the time.

But afterwards she told us that she was about to go under—John was working on her hiatus hernia and migraine—she'd seen a vivid orange flash.

Her husband had appeared to her, and she'd wanted to cry out his name and talk to him, but didn't want to frighten my wife.

We had noticed that she hadn't seemed able to relax properly. It was almost as if she was resisting treatment, and now we knew why.

Even so, John had somehow managed to discover what we had not told him—that my mother-in-law had had eye and ear trouble in the past.

My wife had only come along to keep us company, but John was anxious to see if she would be a good subject.

Just as she was going under, she cried out as if in sudden pain.

She told us afterwards that she had been startled by the sight of a bright orange ball hurtling towards her, and by a tremendous force she felt was pushing her back on to the couch.

Then she felt her father's presence in the room. She wanted to speak to him, but couldn't "get through".

This was before her mother and I had talked of our own experiences.

After the initial shock, she relaxed completely and drifted off very deeply. It didn't take John long to discover that she had leg trouble. In fact, she suffers from rheumatism stemming from a childhood illness.

Without actually touching her legs, he ran his healing hands up and down them a few inches away. She came to with intense pins and needles in her feet, a sensation I also had noticed in mine.

My mother-in-law so far has been free of migraines. But three days after the session she had "terrible pains in the stomach—like pins and needles".

John Cain commented: "It sounds like she's having dispersal pains—a sort of healing crisis".

My wife has had no trouble with her legs. And for the first time in years she's able to keep them still in bed.

But whatever the long-term effects of that healing session, I have got to admit than an afternoon with the remarkable John Cain has given this cynic something to think about as he massages his bad back."

Articles about me did not only appear in local or national newspapers and magazines but throughout the world. The Kuwait daily newspaper ran a series on me in 1984; I believe it was that edition in arabic which actually painted a moustache on my face, probably to make me look more Middle Eastern. The main subject in their edition of the 5th September was a lady called Cathy Rodgers (42); her case history was extensively reported, and speaking of her response to my healing she was quoted as saying ". . . that night my stomach felt numb. The next day I noticed that the skin outside had turned deep red and it was in a ridge, just like an operation scar. The next day the scar was gone and I an now completely cured. . ."

There appears to have been press wide coverage in the Middle East, and I even had on one occasion a Rolls Royce draw up at my front door with several Middle Eastern gentlemen. They turned out to be aides and secretaries of a very important Sheik, who was awaiting an operation in a private London clinic. It appears that he had read about me, including one of those usual "personality profiles" which are the product of some writer's fertile imagination. As far as I could make out the Sheik had read that I drank whiskey by the bottle and smoked cigarettes by the carton; on the other hand I would never accept a penny for my services. I am used to surprises but I admit to great astonishment when the Arabic gentleman unloaded a huge crate of whiskey bottles and God knows how many cartons of American cigarettes. They then handed me an envelope containing bank notes to cover my travelling and hotel expenses and demanded that I follow them to London the next day as their Lord and Master was refusing to undergo an urgently needed operation without my telling him that he should do so. Because of his eminent position his wealth and power the surgeons looked on helplessly because the Sheik could have easily changed clinics if they had not complied with his wishes for 'a second opinion'. Let me add here that I was greeted with great courtesy by all when I arrived at the clinic the next day, and I remember the relief on the faces of the surgeons and doctors when I told him (and I did so because I knew it was the right thing to do) that he should consent to the operations without delay. The Sheik merely insisted that I remained in London and see him once more after the operation. He seemed to take healing for granted and I am sure that he never distinguished between the advice given him by the eminent surgeons of Harley Street and my one sentence: "you are going to have that operation right away".

I don't think I have ever suffered a 'bad press'. Whenever journalists or reporters wanted to be present at a healing session I agreed; when I was asked for an interview I spoke to them, but I never put on any airs or tried to impress them with hollow claims, which perhaps accounts for the same theme running through most headlines or sub-titles

LIVERPOOL ECHO

"Crippled for years, within minutes the woman was able to walk around the room. Miracle or myth it is a mystery".

THE GUARDIAN

"The age of miracles is not yet passed".

NEWS OF THE WORLD

"Today doctors, psychiatrists, scientists and churchmen are talking about John Cain."

OBSERVER

"No sanctimonious man this, but certainly an extraordinary one".

I find it singularly difficult to write about myself and especially about my successes as a healer. It is for this reason that I return once more to the two half hour long radio programmes "Beyond Belief" with Kieran Devaney. I am extracting from four of the interviews which were conducted by Mr Devaney. I had more mail and enquiries about these than any other; perhaps it has something to do with the type of illness but especially the unmistakable sincerity with which these four people told their stories.

Miss Valerie Jones, a young theatre director from Cheshire, diagnosed to be suffering from Multiple Sclerosis following a most serious car accident and having undergone four years of major and painful operations:

"I had been feeling quite rough for some time. I was lying with my head on my hand and got pins and needles in my fingers; the only unusual thing at that point was that they did not go away. Within two hours it was right down the right hand side of me. The 'pins and needles' lasted two or three days and were followed first by a complete numbness and then a total collapse on one side.

I was paralysed! I had lost the will to live. I knew that nothing was going to work for me. . . ''

'' . . . John came himself, and I did not know what was happening to me.

All I knew was that *something* was happening. The doctors, the drugs and all the other methods which had been attempted to bring about an improvement had had no effect on me whatever; in fact, the drugs actually made my condition worse. By the time I left John Cain that evening I *knew* I would get better.''

"Where would I be now without John Cain?"

"I would be dead!"

Mrs Sheila Spears of Liverpool, was another interviewee. Seven years ago she had been crippled with an incurable cancer, dying an agonising death. "I was bedridden, on Pethidine tablets (which are now prescribed instead of morphine and taken for the most severe pain), sleeping tablets, Triptosol tablets, which are strong tablets to affect the nervous system, and yet I never slept. I was just like a dying animal, that is the only way to describe me, I looked a hundred years old and was partly bent in two. As I was coming out, the sweat was literally bucketing from me due to the pain. Somebody said "get John" and all I could hear was "Get John, John will see you." I was more or less saying to my sister "let's get the hell out of here". Anyway, this John came out and knelt beside me and he asked me to close my eyes. My actual words to him were "On your way mate. Bugger off away from me, you or no-one else can help me"; I just swore at him, he told me to close my eyes because I was crying with pain. My sister told me to close my eyes, and just to please her I did so. All John did was kneel at my side; he asked our kid which side the pain was on, then John just placed one hand on my back and the other on my left thigh. Within 60 seconds, it was just like a finger entering into my spine and a light switch being switched off. I just said: "you've got it, its gone. Mate, you don't know what the bloody hell has happened here tonight." Because I immediately sat up straight on the chair, my sister started screaming. [Here Sheila Spears began to cry]. I just can't talk about it, Kieran, without being amazed; if anyone asks me to talk about it, I can't without getting all choked up. If I were to die tomorrow I have been given maybe seven years from this man, which I never even had as a young girl.

"I walked out of that hall, got into my sister's car and then out again; I did that four times just for the novelty of being able to get in and out of a car on my own.

"When, several months later, we stopped at the chemist for the drugs, he asked my husband Douglas: "Mr Spears, I am frightened to ask you, but where is Mrs Spears?" Douglas said: "she is fine", and the chemist replied "I was so worried because you have not been coming here for the drugs." He actually thought I had died.

The case of Mrs Violet Bloomfield of Chingford was presented slightly differently. Much of the evidence which had been obtained and which supported the claims which were made consisted of actual letters from Mrs Bloomfield's medical file. Although these were read out with the names of surgeons and doctors concerned with her case, my publishers feel that it would be unwise to publish the names of writers or recipients of letters because of the question of copyright involved. However, as the original letters and the medical files of Violet Bloomfield are available for inspection, there is no reason not to extract from the content of the letters what is relevant to the claims which have been made.

This is how Mrs Bloomfield's case was presented:

"Violet Bloomfield's condition is no ordinary one; her nerves are bad because four years ago a doctor diagnosed cancer of the bowel and told her she had less than twelve months to live. We have obtained evidence which supports this claim. Violet Bloomfield's own medical file contains, among others, this letter from a surgeon:

'. . . . . . . Hospital, London E11.

Dear N.,

With reference to Violet Bloomfield, date of birth 26 July 1941, 74 Chingford Avenue, London E4: This patient was seen in June of this year complaining of lower abdominal pain and dyspareunia and was thought to have an ovarian cyst in the Pouch of Douglas and was therefore admitted for a laporotomy as a waiting-list-case. She had a laporotomy on 15 July and was found to have an anterior rectal carcinoma involving her right utero-sacral ligaments.

We discussed this problem with one surgical colleague and he feels that this inoperable. Both the patient and her husband have been informed of the diagnosis and the prognosis which we feel must be less than a year.

Yours sincerely, N.N. Registrar to Mr N. Consultant Gynaecologist.'

Violet Bloomfield was shaken and stunned, [at this point she takes up her own story].

"My first reaction was that they had made a mistake, but they had cut me open and obviously seen something and they had it tested. But I still said they made a mistake. He said: 'No, we have not made a mistake, that doctor is a very good doctor, he knows what he is doing'. I was floored, I just couldn't believe it. It just didn't sink in. I was condemned to a slow agonishing death from an incurable illness. They proposed to prescribe a Brompton Cocktail, a strong concoction of heroin and pethidine to ease my last days.'

Then Violet Bloomfield read about John Cain.

"I felt a lot happier when I came back. We started going up there once a month or when we could make it, for three or four days at a time. Everyone said to me each time I came home, how much better I looked."

Two years later, twelve months after she should have been dead, Violet Bloomfield returned to the hospital where her incurable illness had been originally diagnosed. Her medical file reveals this amazing letter:

'. . . . . . Hospital, London E11.

20 September 1982.

Dear Mr N.

With reference to Violet Bloomfield, date of birth 26 July 1941, 74 Chingford Avenue, London E4: This patient was operated on by my Registrar some two years ago, and he found what he thought was inoperable carcinoma of the rectum, confirmed to be an adeno carcinoma from an endoscopic biopsy I examined her today, two years later, she is fit and well and putting on weight. I do believe the diagnosis was wrong in the first instance and I am asking N. N. to see her for re-assessment.

Yours sincerely, N. N. Consultant Gynaecologist.'

[Here Mrs Bloomfield takes up the story]

"The doctors put it aside; They poo-pooed it all. One doctor was quite nice; he said 'well, I can't help thinking that your *doctor* up in Liverpool has got all the credit for this'. My own family doctor was quite sarcastic and said 'why don't I go to my other "*doctor*" up in Liverpool".

"Violet Bloomfield's re-examination showed no trace of cancer. Today she lives a normal life. Violet Bloomfield believes she was cured by John Cain. Her doctors remain unbelieving. Their scepticism is common among their profession: even Liverpool's community health expert, Dr John Ashton will tell you that cures like that just don't happen.

'I think most healers are presumably well-meaning and well-intentioned, but I would be concerned that some of them probably extract money from people who cannot afford it and that they would be raising hopes of people when there is no cause for that, but probably, most importantly, that people might be distracted from properly trained, scientifically trained doctors, who have gone to great pains to acquire their skills and who are using methods of treatment which have been tried and scientifically evaluated, whereas, of course, these methods have not been.'

"Do you think there is anything in it?"

'I personally don't.'

[The next voice is that of a family doctor who has been sending patients to John Cain]

"He (John Cain) is certainly a tremendous force for good in my opinion, in medicine."

"Dr Michael Azurdia is a Wirral General Practitioner. He is the leading campaigner in raising money for cancer research at Clatterbridge Hospital. What makes him different is that while most doctors scorn the work of John Cain, the healer, Dr Azurdia actually shares his patients with him.

Dr Azurdia:

"A number of patients have said that they go to him regularly or irregularly and they do seem to derive an awful lot of relief and solace from his help. A patient of mine, whom I didn't know what to do with, she had reached the end of the line with investigation and treatment, I had to tell honestly that I didn't feel I could help her any more; but I did feel that she could be helped by someone like John Cain, and that she really ought to go along and see him. She went along to see John and the very next day she rang me to say how much better she was feeling as a result of her visit to him.

"Since that time I have seen her on one occasion for a very minor ailment and I understand that she has derived an enormous help from John Cain and has been very well.

"Since this episode, I have subsequently sent a number of patients to him and in almost every case they have been helped.

"I think he is a very remarkable man, and I, like everybody else, cannot understand how he works. But he has that gift to help people. He does get in tune with their thinking habits and thought processes, and a definite improvement in their health ensues as a result of his intervention. He has never hurt anybody, he does not ask for money, he does manage to help his patients enormously, and I must say he is certainly a tremendous force for good in medicine in my opinion."

CHAPTER 2

REFLECTIONS OF JOHN CAIN: FUTURE POSSIBILITIES

SINCE first realising that I had these 'extraordinary powers' I have searched for a possible answer and I will continue to search as long as people are in need of help.

All people undergo the continuous evolution towards a total consciousness and I believe that is the reason why we are in this realm. Everything is the result of cause and effect; and in the same way man is evolving on many levels, so does healing evolve and change.

Between 1981 when the *JOHN CAIN HEALING GUIDE* was published and 1985 my method of healing has somewhat changed from that described in the guide. Perhaps it is best described as something more approaching the true spiritual level.

Of course there have been writings, going back to the earliest manuscripts which make reference to energies that create 'Totally Conscious Beings', a genius, a creative person and many more extraordinarily gifted men and women. The tenor of these writings has not really changed over the millennia, and what is often referred to as 'energies' I prefer to call "Life Force", which is controlled by 'Intelligence'. Others speak of the "Christ Consciousness', and others again of the "Cosmic Mind". It does not matter what terminology we use; there is no doubt in my mind that this "Living Energy" exists beyond the horizon of our intellectual understanding.

People follow certain paths to raise their awareness to become enlightened or gain an experience. They often do so without realising that beyond their own minds there is a Divine Will and that a Divine Intelligence is always there and ever-present in what we think, say or do.

I believe that the 'Intelligence' is responsible for the healing and that I am a medium between the 'Life Force' and those people who are in need.

My reason for developing the 'Life Force' with the co-operation of certain receptive helpers is to ensure that this powerful energy can be used to help as many people as possible. The physical manipulation of patients has been reduced to a minimum and another, more beneficial way has been found to utilise the 'Healing Intelligence''.

Many of my patients, both individually and collectively, seem to have developed a far higher awareness of love which accompanies the "physical healing". Patients find that relaxation is almost immediate, their minds are at ease and they experience a rapport with something which they describe as "feeling good". There have been a number of cases where patients spoke of 'experiencing colour' and even cases of clairvoyance have been known, depending on the patient's receptiveness.

I believe that the 'Life Force' is responsible for these manifestations and, in fact, for all the other paranormal phenomena and enlightenment. It is true to say that one can only regard such happenings as genuine when they are accompanied by certain personality changes.

Of course, the use of the 'Life Force' in my healing method is of relatively recent origin and I am confident that it will continue to develop for many years to come. Perhaps later this year I shall be writing in greater detail about the 'Life Force' and the experiences receptive people have had and are continuing to have. I very much hope that I will be able to publish this towards the end of 1985. However, it would be misleading to assume that the 'receptive' people were 'receptive' when they joined us for the first time. Receptiveness, like everything else, develops in time.

John Cain with Doreen Thomas whose Kundalini poetry and prose has astonished everybody. Her work is consistently improving in quality and quantity.

I have noticed over the last few years how the attitude of my patients has changed; they are far more aware; they desire to reach a higher consciousness, experience higher emotions of love and understanding, and to progress. I have met many who have made remarkable progress in a very short time, like Doreen Thomas who writes remarkable poetry.*

It is quite obvious that more and more patients are in search of a 'higher self' and I am confident that with a concerted help of the 'Life Force' this can be achieved, at least to some larger extent.

At the Healing Centre we use the scientific instruments known as 'Mind Mirrors' in an attempt to ascertain what precisely is happening to some of the patients. This method does not enable us to monitor the 'Living Energy' or 'Higher Intelligence'; but it measures accurately the reactions of patients in the altered state of consciousness during healing. Naturally different people respond differently but generally speaking the altered state of consciousness needs to be relatively slight and only strong

* see Appendix for three of the poems by Doreen Thomas.

enough to allow the 'Life Force' to permeate the various levels of the person's consciousness.

I have already mentioned that in the altered state of consciousness, once it permeates a person's different levels of consciousness, experiences apart from physical warmth or heat, often associated with 'physical healing' also and more consistently now, a highter spiritual love and tranquility. I have been particularly impressed with the creativity it seems to evoke. For example, I have known people to write poetry and in doing so reducing stress and outward pressures on them.

This energy seems to last longer as time goes on.

The John Cain Healing Centre published its own regular newsletter **KIT** (Keeping in Touch). Because of the ever-increasing number of patients, friends and supporters it had become necessary to produce means of communication. For example, the demand for the book *HEAL, MY SON!* was so great that I had no choice but to have it reprinted. However, because it was written eight years ago, it is necessary to add some of the many things which have happened since then. The book, *YOU DON'T KNOW JOHN CAIN?* is, in a manner of speaking, timeless because it is an impressive list of case histories. These have proved particularly beneficial to those who were new to healing and apprehensive about the subject. The *JOHN CAIN HEALING GUIDE* was not so much a DIY guide to healing as a companion for those who will link in regularly during my absent healing sessions. It also described possible symptoms and reactions, particularly in the altered state of consciousness, and Valerie Wooding gave an almost minute by minute account of the process of healing, entering into the altered state of consciousness, experiencing temperature changes, manipulations, vibrations and emotional release. I explained earlier that I have reduced manipulation to a minimum because I found the alternative method more successful and beneficial. Nevertheless, the *HEALING GUIDE* has been and will continue to be of enormous help to those who cannot visit the Healing Centre in Birkenhead.

I regard my forthcoming book I am writing at this moment which deals with the 'Life Force' as my most important work yet; it deals with the most important evolution in healing and

I am most anxious to communicate to all those who wish to benefit from it the varied aspects and properties of the 'Life Force' (known as the *KUNDALINI* in Eastern cultures, and as we know it in the field of healing.)

There have been already several accounts, written by patients and friends who experienced *KUNDALINI*. One we published in our newsletter, the others were sent directly to my friend and close collaborator, Norman Carter, who co-ordinates many of my activities. To give the reader an introductory idea of the *KUNDALINI* experience, these accounts have been reproduced in the next chapter.

CHAPTER 3

'EXPERIENCES THROUGH THE LIFE FORCE'

I

JIM KEMP – Sydney – Australia. [Reprinted from KIT, Summer 1982].

"I had felt restless for some time, not knowing what I was seeking, but I knew that whatever it was it lay outside of my normal haunts. This feeling of uncertainty and dissatisfaction grew daily, so fifteen years ago I made the decision to leave the Wirral and go to Australia. I had numerous occupations in Australia until I met a Mr George Ogilvie who introduced me to Siddha Meditation. I had always shunned Yoga and meditation before, but the feeling of there being something 'in it' was getting too strong to ignore.

"I practiced Siddha Meditation for 18 months during which time I received *"Shaktipat"* or transmission of spiritual energy. During this transmission there was a feeling of enormous energy entering the system and a feeling of great age and intelligence.

"It was at the end of this 18 months period that I learned that my mother in England had cancer, but my passport had expired and I did not have enough money, and no plane was available. But as soon as I followed the feeling of returning to England, everything fell into place. People appeared from nowhere offering me money and my flight was booked. I arrived home within a week. I had never heard of John Cain, but my brother and mother had been to visit him, so I accompanied her on her next visit.

"To my astonishment the feeling of the 'energy' in John Cain's Healing Centre was exactly the same as the Ashram in Sydney; it did not stop there. For the first time that John laid hands on me, I felt the same energy as I had in "Shaktipat" but much more purposely now, more direct, more specifically controlled. I immediately began to feel the energy rising up in the region of my spine. I now had the feeling that I had been led to John Cain's Healing Centre.

"Some weeks later I attended a demonstration of the raising of the 'Life Force' for Dr D. Blything, Lecturer in Psychology.

"The energy released in me was the strongest so far experienced. It was getting progressively deeper and higher until I found that my heart felt as though it was opening and I was suddenly completely enveloped in myself and I experienced the most euphoric, ecstatic and releasing feeling that I have ever known. I felt as if I were at least free in my own true nature. I could do anything, there was no barrier between myself and me. I knew what was meant by "Holy Spirit"; every mystical cliché finally made sense, the light was blue with flashing gold – the present was endless. Suffice it to say, I went round the world, but the moment of realisation actually arrived through the grace of John Cain, just three miles away from where I was born – back in my own backyard."

II

DORIS HOLMES, Bromborough, Wirral.

"I first met John Cain on the recommendation of Vincent Rylance, the Head of Yoga International. My first meeting with John Cain was at a healing session and I was wearing a collar to support my neck. My neck felt a little easier after one of the helpers had laid his hands on the back of my neck and gently stretched the neck. I found myself shedding tears, not uncommon in healing. Prior to the general healing, John Cain gently massaged my neck, and I went home that night with a feeling of deep inner peace. At my second session I began to have massage and manipulation: it was so painful but I felt my back muscles being moved in a way which would be impossible to do myself. At my next meeting I was thrown forward by some force into a sitting position, my back stretched, my head pushed towards my knees and my arms stretched forward, and my hands back under my feet. A position I recognised but probably more advanced than I had experienced ever before. Next, my arms were stretched out either side of my body, then I was spun over and pressed to the floor. But the climax was being pushed up into a 'camel-backward-bending-posture' which, under normal conditions I would find very hard to do. Yet I was almost lifted into this and several other positions, finishing with a 'Cobra', an excellent exercise for back problems and surely the best that I have ever experienced.

"I stayed for the raising of the 'Life Force' demonstration in which I was to take part. John touched the base of my spine, and then the body started to speak. I was discerning a voice in my ear, explaining the story of the Yoga beliefs. My hands pressed over the *chakra* centres of my body. My hands were finally moved to the neck. The inner voice said *Shiva* and *Shakti* which symbolises that the 'Life Force' has been aroused, and I felt a great over-flowing feeling of affinity and felt as if I were singing inside. I was singing over and over again the chant "You are beautiful to my heart". I felt a one-ness with the 'Universal Consciousness' and I felt at peace.

"I no longer wear the neck collar and feel much better. All I can add is that if you see someone else whilst having healing, doing these movements, you will be able to appreciate what I have told you. They have reached a spark of God, said to dwell in the heart of all his creatures, and they are growing into spiritual awareness."

III

SHELAGH MAUDSLEY, Aintree, Liverpool.

"Life begins with birth but my life began with John Cain and experiences in life very few people are privileged to have. It is the quality of life that counts.

"Two years ago I suffered from nervous stress. I was gradually but completely losing interest in life, my home, my family and job. I knew I had to shake myself out of it, but how to go about it was the question I had asked myself for months.

"John Cain was obviously the answer; but I was a sceptic and initially did not want to know. Sitting in my lounge one evening, feeling my usual depressed self, I picked up a book about John which my mother had left for me to read. The photograph on the front cover had drawn my attention to the book. As I looked at the photograph, to my amazement it changed, and all I could see was a Chinese looking at me, drawing me closer and telling me to seek healing. I did the very next day, and since then I have never looked back.

"My first experience of Kundalini, or raising the 'Life Force' as we know it, was to fight and try to overpower this restlessness that burned inside in me. I soon learned it was much easier to accept the energy and power given out by the 'Life Force', not only to help me on the road to recovery but also to help John Cain with his valuable work of healing, than to resist it.

"My experiences since that first encounter have been many and wonderful. I have had the experience of being drawn so close to John's picture in the healing room that I have felt as though I have walked through it, and off this earth into gardens so green they belong to another, far-off place. I have witnessed the most wonderful colours which cannot possibly belong on this earth. I have experienced within myself a love so wonderful, a peace so calm and a feeling of a real privilege of experiencing the 'Life Force'. Through guidance I have written poetry, which could only be written with help from another source, far greater than we have here on earth. The power of the 'Life Force' exists in all, but for the few that can be made aware of it, many people can be helped and healed each hour of every day. My life has taken on a new meaning: a healing, caring and peaceful meaning which, when the power and work of the Kundalini is recognised, will make our earth a healthier, happier and more peaceful place to live in.

CHAPTER 4

PAT ASHFORD

"It is now twelve months since I first went to see John Cain at work at a healing session in Blackrod. I took my mother one Sunday night because no-one else was available to take her; she seemed to be deriving some benefit from her visits. When I say I went to *see* John Cain at work, that is precisely what I meant. I had no intention of becoming involved in any way. I merely took my mother and intended to watch. I watched with an extremely critical eye; so cynical was I, that John Cain (so he has told me since) picked up my thoughts and vowed that no way was he coming to me. However, as the evening progressed John started his '*beam out*', and as he did so I was literally flung backwards in my chair so strongly that I thought I would fall. I went immediately into an altered state of consciousness and was gently led to a bed by one of the helpers. I felt my body go light and floaty and I just couldn't keep still. I don't know how long I lay there, but after a while someone (I know it was John) came and put his hands on my solar plexus, and I now quote from my diary entry of Sunday, 12 August 1984. 'At the first touch I felt like an electric current had gone through me, I could feel surges of energy coming from him to me all through my back so powerfully I couldn't keep still. It was absolutely ecstatic, honestly, I feel so hightly charged with energy I don't know what to do with myself.'

"Almost twelve months on I can still say that I will never

be the same again. I have changed beyond recognition and I am still having the most amazing experiences, some of which I will relate with the help of my diary. Before I begin I would just like to say that I am still fully charged with energy – revving like an overtuned engine at times – I need much less sleep and feel so positive, I feel I could cope with almost anything that life throws at me. I have also changed into a much more sensitive and generally more aware sort of person. I feel a certain empathy when dealing with people and feel much more loving as a result. I can tolerate things which used to irritate me and feel very moved when dealing with sickness.

"I am now aware of God and an 'Higher Intelligence', and feel I am never alone. I am aware of life, space, nature, energy, health and healing and above all, love. The love I feel when taking part in the healing sessions is so powerful it takes my breath away at times.

"After the August 12th incident, I didn't attend another session until September 2nd because of my summer holiday.

"My diary entry for 2 September reads amongst other things: 'I took my mother to John Cain again tonight and had a more powerful experience than before, I will never be the same again. John put his hands on certain points on my spine and made me so high I felt I was going through the roof. John himself said that Yogis take 30 years to experience what I had just experienced. It was absolutely wonderful.' I have remained as high as a kite ever since except for two occasions which I will describe later.

"From 2 September I have attended the sessions as regularly as possible and even though I continue to have these wonderful experiences, I often attend taking with me an element of doubt and cynicism. I sometimes go and think to myself – this is a test week – I will not be involved at all, but as soon as John passes my chair I am out like a light. I have thought it might have something to do with hypnotism or guided fantasy, but how can I be in a state of hypnosis week in and week out? And how can it be guided fantasy when John does not say a word, and if there is nothing why I should register such strange patterns from my brain on a machine designed to measure brain activity. My entry on 16 September: 'He (John) wired me up to a machine which measures the activity of the brain and started a session with me. He said the activity was fantastic and beautiful and that I had achieved something that only a handful of people had ever achieved. He reckoned that at one point my brain activity ceased, indicating that for a few seconds I was 'clinically' dead. I was just aware all the time of one-ness, love, warmth and ecstasy.' This was very convincing and surely had nothing to do with trickery, hypnosis or whatever.

"Time and time again, my entries say: 'where do I go from here? What is it all for?' I have no answers, except that I do know I am being used by some wonderful power, and as the weeks have progressed, I have found that I have been able to use this power myself. I did not realise that I could, until in January 1985, when I was shown it by a 'Higher Intelligence' in a most incredible way – without any conscious thought at all. I had taken my mother to see John at the Healing Centre in North Road, Birkenhead, during the Christmas holidays and I had a session myself. I felt like I always do after a session, really good, relaxed and carefree; but during the following weekend, I came down to earth with a bang. I felt weepy and depressed and irritable. I decided it was because I had been feeling ill with a headache, feelings of tightness and soreness in my chest and a bad cough. Moreover, I also found that I could not link in with John, and I had been able to do that at will since the very first time I had attended his sessions. Three or four days passed before I could link in again, but this time not very strongly. Two more things happened during that week.

"One morning, around 3–4 am, I woke up strongly feeling I had given John Cain a healing session. A day or two later, I woke up quite early in the morning again, this time having dreamt that somebody had telephoned and asked me to go to Liverpool to see John. I actually went there in my dream but I have no recollection how I got there or where exactly I went. I entered a room which was quite dark and I saw John Cain was breathing heavily and asleep. I remember seeing a green colour and there were three or four other people present. I really don't know what happened; I just remember going. Norman Carter telephoned me that evening and told me that John Cain had left hospital and was feeling much better after having suffered a serious heart attack.

"It was probably from then on that I felt that if I could be used in a dream for healing (and I do not really know whether I was or not) then I could possibly be used conciously as well. I started giving my Mother regular sessions which she says really helped. She has suffered a tremendous amount of pain from various ulcers (one on each ankle), and she says that after I have laid my hands on them, the pain had eased considerably, and a side effect is that she sleeps well too.

"I do not know why, but if I have been asked to help, the result seems more dramatic, and I feel the energy flowing through me much more strongly; likewise when I ask for help (for myself). My sister suffers from migraine, and on two occasions has telephoned and asked if I could help. Both times, as she was speaking to me, I have experienced powerful serges of energy flowing through me and my heart-beat starting to race. I consciously thought of her headache being lifted and visualised it taking place. I left it at that point and after an hour or so, she telephoned to say the headache had gone. I knew before it rang that it had, because the first time I tried, I picked up her headache and then an hour later, mine faded and I was left with a tremendous feeling of peace and well being.

"Another incident was when I was asked for help and received it in abundance. Mother was ill, and my sister and I were taking it in turns to telephone her each morning and evening to make sure she was all right. One Friday night it was my turn and I rang as usual; there was no reply. I rang again later – and again later – nothing. At this stage, I was feeling quite worried and finally rang my sister to find out if she knew anything. She said she had visited Mother earlier and Mother had said she felt so tired she had decided to have an early night – I stopped worrying. The next morning, at about 9 o'clock, I telephoned again – no answer. At 9.30 and 10 a.m. I rang again – no answer. I began to panic but left it until 10.30 – still no reply. By this time I was frantic and decided I would have to go and see her (this is a 40 minutes drive). Just before I left, however, I sat down in the kitchen and prayed that if anyone was with me spiritually, would they please go and see that my Mother was all right. Within 10 minutes I had my answer – I felt a perfect peace and calm and love enveloped me. I rang Mother's number again. Not only did she answer, but instead of giving her own number 691187, she said 'hello 56825' which is my number! The explanation was that she had gone to bed early, very tired, and had slept until the early hours when she woke up because her legs were hurting. She had finally dropped off to sleep again and woke up around 11 a.m. feeling much better.

"More recently (early July 1985) I had another wonderful experience. My elder sister had to go into hospital suddenly for an operation. When I knew the time of her operation, I immediately rang John and asked him to "beam out" to her. He picked up the telephone as if he had been expecting me to ring, and before I had said a word he said "it is 2 o'clock this afternoon – she will be all right – no complications – no worries – I will be right with her". He was right, it was straightforward, no complications and my sister had her operation without a care in the world. She is now recovering very quickly and is convinced it is because of the spiritual support she received.

"An interesting factor about this incident is that before I had rung the hospital and John Cain, I had been trying to send some thoughts out to her. I had also tried to send Mother some thoughts, and to an aunt and uncle (both in hospital) and a friend who is also desperately ill. As I was doing this, I felt my energy fading and I ended up feeling absolutely and totally drained, exhausted and quite weepy. When I rang John about my sister, I was still feeling quite weary, so he told me to go and lie down and immediately link in with him. I went upstairs, laid down, and within seconds I felt as if my back was lifted from the bed. As I floated I was surrounded by waves of green, orange, gold and a beautiful purple blue. The telephone and the children disturbed me, or I reckon I would have stayed there all day, but when I did get up 10 minutes later, I was back to normal: in high spirits, energetic and a lot happier. During the course of that day my spine was manipulated on a number of occasions at different points from the base right up to my neck. I literally rose higher and higher as the day went on. (These spinal manipulations are not new to me; they started at my first session and have happened regularly).

"More recently, however, I have also had a feeling of a swelling in my throat and pressure on my temples at the same time.

"Finally, I have said that I never feel I am alone, mainly because I have been able to ask for help and have received it in all sorts of different ways. But even when I have not asked, there has been guidance, never more marked than when I was coming home from a healing session some weeks ago. I had come away feeling quite intoxicated. As I drove on to the motorway (which is only a couple of miles away from the Community Centre) my car temperatue gauge suddenly shot up. It went right up to the red danger zone. I moved over onto the hard shoulder and stopped. I had to wait about 10 minutes before it gradually moved down. By this time I felt quite calm and travelled home safely, having done nothing to the heater and it has not over-heated since. I have also been a lot more careful since then and have made quite sure the after-effects of the healing session had worn off before driving my car.

"I am still asking the question "where do I go from here" but don't worry too much about it now. I am sure that all will be revealed in time. In any case, if I never have another experience again for the rest of my life, what I have experienced during the last year is with me and is a part of me for ever. I feel extremely privileged to have been able to have been involved.

CHAPTER 5

NUALA COULSTON

I first heard about John Cain and his healing through a friend of mine, Christine. She spoke to me about the 'Kundalini Energy' of which I knew absolutely nothing. I was fascinated

Mrs. Pat Ashford and Mrs. Nuala Coulston, two of John Cain's most promising Kundalini students; both have benefitted greatly from Kundalini and given an account of their experiences here.

and I felt sufficiently drawn to it that one Sunday evening I went along with her to the Blackrod Community Centre where the healing sessions were taking place. It was all very new to me. I had never experienced any type of healing before. The first thing that struck me was the feeling of peace in the hall, but it was not at all as I had expected. It seemed like a dance hall, with soft music playing and everyone sitting around tables having what seemed endless cups of tea. I kept expecting someone to come over and ask me for the next dance. The atmosphere was very tranquil and I could feel myself drifting and becoming very 'floaty'! I can remember that when I walked, the floor seemed 'springy' or as if I was walking on air. I know now that I was going into an altered state of consciousness, but I did not know what was happening to me at the time.

Eventually we were asked to take a bed. I lay down next to my friend. I had no clue what would happen next, and I suppose I felt a little nervous. I soon became very relaxed and slipped into a very peaceful and tranquil state. I was bathed in deep blue and purple pulsating lights. I think I could have stayed there forever; it was so beautiful and I was filled with a feeling of great love and harmony. When I eventually came round, I was absolutely amazed at how much time had gone by. Later the same evening, sitting at the side, I witnessed something which took my breath away and held me spellbound. Several 'Kundalinis' formed a circle with John in the centre. The whole thing looked like a flower opening up its petals. It was beautiful. I did not have the faintest idea what was happening, but somewhere deep in side me I knew that this was the place where I belonged.

The second time I went to a healing session, John Cain laid his hands on my spine. I began to feel that incredible vibrating energy permeating throughout the whole of my being. It was so strong, it was almost painful. I remember feeling tremendous strength in my arms. My whole body felt as though it was pulsating, taking my breath away, and my heart seemed to be racing one minute missing beats the next and at some points seemed to stop altogether. This was the beginning of the 'Kundalini energy' being raised in me and from that time onwards it has gone from strength to strength.

"One of my early experiences of this energy came about three weeks after I first went to see John Cain. I had just gone to bed when these tremendous sensations were literally spiraling throughout the whole of my body, right from the tips of my toes to the top of my head and beyond and then back again. This repeated itself over and over again. At the same time I felt as though I was whirling through space, seeing flashes of light. It was as though I was travelling around the Universe. Words cannot fully express that tremendous experience. That experience made me realise that John's touch had sparked something off in me from which there was no return. I did not understand any of it. I did not know what direction my life would take, or what it was all about; I felt the same as that first night at Blackrod; that this was where I belonged. This was my natural path. Of course, I did have the choice of whether to absorb all this into my mind and I faced a lot of opposition to it at that time. Nevertheless, I kept taking that next step, seeing John Cain each Sunday evening at the Community Centre. Doubts melted away and questions were answered. Something very deep inside of me was urging me on.

Apart from these wonderful experiences bringing me great joy and unity, not only within myself but with the world around me, the greatest joy for me is to be used to give this love to others. I have always wanted to help others in need and now I have the opportunity to pass on something so wonderful. It took me quite a long time to realise that I could give what I was receiving to other people, and I did not really have the confidence to try.

In February 1984, my husband received a very serious blow to his head, causing a fractured skull and some brain damage. The Consultant did not give me much hope for his life. Whilst he was in the operating theatre, I telephoned John Cain to ask for his help. John started to beam out healing straight away and said that he would do so every hour and he also said that he would link in with me at certain times each day so that he could transmit his healing through me to my husband, while I was at his bedside.

"These were wonderful experiences for me because I felt the presence of John Cain very close during this very stressful time. I knew when he was linking in with me because I became very still and peaceful inside. I could feel the energy pulsating up my spine when giving healing to my husband. John also visited my husband in hospital on two occasions. The first time was only a couple of days after the accident. My husband's head, the side of his face and eye were very swollen and bruised. John laid his hands on him during a healing session, and within three days, most of the swelling and bruising had gone. My husband reported later that he had felt wonderful warmth in this area of his body. The nurses and doctors were absolutely amazed at his progress. During my visits to the hospital, I became more confident that this healing energy could be passed on through me. A man in the same ward as my husband had shown interest in what we were doing, and I could see he was in great pain. I offered to give him some healing for his back. I put my hands under his spine and I felt movements in my own back and stomach as the energy was being drawn through me. My hands went extremely hot, almost as if I had them on a radiator. I noticed that the man started to sweat, great beads of sweat rolled down his face. I knew something was happening. Afterwards he said he felt fantastic, the pain had gone, and he said he still felt a great deal of heat in his back. I gave him one of John's books to read and suggested that he should get in touch with him when he came out of hospital but I don't know whether he ever did. I will never be able to thank John enough for the help that he freely gave at that very distressing time.

I continued with the healing sessions every Sunday night at the Blackrod Community Centre; there was no keeping me away now. The scenery along this path was too beautiful to miss, the flowers, the trees and the birds singing, the grass, the sky, the clouds, the stars, even the air I was breathing, all pulsating with the same energy, all singing the praises of a Higher Being; all in tune, all perfect. While on this path, I feel in tune with it; if I strayed from it, I would be lost. I now feel part of something which is so immense, it is beyond words. I feel protected. I feel so much love; the kind of love that has no reason, just love.

"At this stage I was asked by John Cain to keep a written record of my experiences and I am now going to recount some of them, but as I have said before, words are inadequate to express the full feeling behind them.

"Tuesday, 28 May, evening, as I lay in bed, tremendous sensations gripped my body. It was incredibly strong. The strongest of the sensations I experienced were in my head, but I could also feel waves of energy up my spine and I was vaguely aware of gentle movement in my back. The sensation in my head was so powerful it almost obliterated every other feeling in my body. There was an almost unbearable ringing and buzzing sound filling my head, and my mouth, particularly my top gum, felt burning hot. I felt a little frightened and I opened my eyes to try and regain some sort of normality. Instead I saw my left arm on the pillow in front of me with a luminous line down each side. I have no idea how long all this lasted, but it gradually subsided and I came back to full consciousness. I related the experience to John Cain and he explained that the 'Kundalini' was probably clearing the throat *chakra*. My hearing has been affected and is now extremely acute.

"Sunday evening, 2 June, during the healing session at Blackrod I experienced the sensation of a waterfall in my head. I could both see and hear it. It was gushing in my head but I was also underneath it, as if there was some dual purpose. It was washing all over me like some sort of cleansing process. Very frequently during the healing sessions, or when I lie down in

The Kundalini Circle in action.

bed, I experience the feeling of being like liquid flowing freely on an undulating floor or mattress.

"Sunday, 9 June, during the healing I felt a tremendous pressure across my forehead and around the area of my temples. My temples also seemed to become very hot, my eyelids felt very irritated and very firmly closed. There was pressure around the back of my eyes. I experienced a complete circle of bright white light in the centre of my forehead and then an eye appeared in the centre of this circle. The circle remained and the eye appeared and disappeared three times during the course of the session.

"Wednesday, 19 June, 3 p.m., I sat down for half an hour or so, not intentionally to meditate. I closed my eyes and I experienced beautiful bright purple lights caressing me. This was going deeper and deeper and it was getting stronger, but unfortunately I was disturbed by my two years old daughter. When I had attended to her, I sat down to resume the experience, but instead of purple light I experienced sparkling white lights showering down, and again I felt as though it could last forever. Again I was disturbed by the children. This experience left me speechless for ten to fifteen minutes and I carried with me a wonderful feeling inside of peace, harmony and well being.

"I could go on forever writing about the wonderful experiences, feelings of peace and joy that I have had since starting at Blackrod just over eighteen months ago. I will instead finish with my latest experience which happened on Thursday, 11 July, during the night.

Again, while lying in bed unable to sleep, tremendous sensations and currents of energy started to surge up my body with great strength, converging in my head.

As before, the sensations in my head were overpowering. They were so strong that I could feel my head being lifted off the pillow with each surge. There were ringing and buzzing sounds again in my head, but this time they became defined and sounded more like a full orchestra tuning up their instruments. This seemed to last quite a while, but then I experienced a complete change of direction of these waves or currents of energy. Until now they had been surging upwards and now, suddenly, they were surging down again. I felt a great pressure as these energies converged at the base of my spine. I was almost like a genie going back into the lamp. The pressure was so strong, it moved me down the bed. The sensations gradually subsided after this, and I slowly came back to normal. My body then felt completely weightless. During this fantastic experience I felt John Cain come to me and put two fingers on my throat and I knew that he could feel what was happening.

I am now completely committed to John Cain's healing work; it is so wonderful, so full of compassion and selfless sacrifice for others.

EPILOGUE

It is far more difficult to add to an existing book than to writing a new book from start. However, as several years had passed since *HEAL, MY SON!* was published, I endeavoured to fill in the reader with the developments which have taken place since then. Also, I am restricted in the number of pages at my disposal because I don't want Part II to distract the reader from the book itself.

Most important, however, was my attempt to sow a seed in the reader's mind: I felt that it would be the right moment to introduce the most important advance and development made in healing: *KUNDALINI*.

As I tried to explain very briefly, there are so many aspects and properties to *KUNDALINI*, so many ways to experience it, benefit from it, and so many paths to follow according to our own choice, that I am convinced that the only direction we shall follow will be the *KUNDALINI* path. It is beyond a question of doubt, that *KUNDALINI* will not only change the reader's life, it will enhance his or her quality of life.

Of course, *KUNDALINI* does not promise you to live longer or attain eternal youth, but it will enrich your life. Once you follow the *KUNDALINI* path, you will no longer be among those who want to live longer but harbour a terror of growing old.

As one of the interviewees so clearly put it: "I had felt restless for some time – not knowing what I was seeking". *KUNDALINI* gave him the answer as it will answer the questions you may have.

John Cain.

Norman Carter, John Cain's friend and collaborator who cordinates many of John Cain's activities.

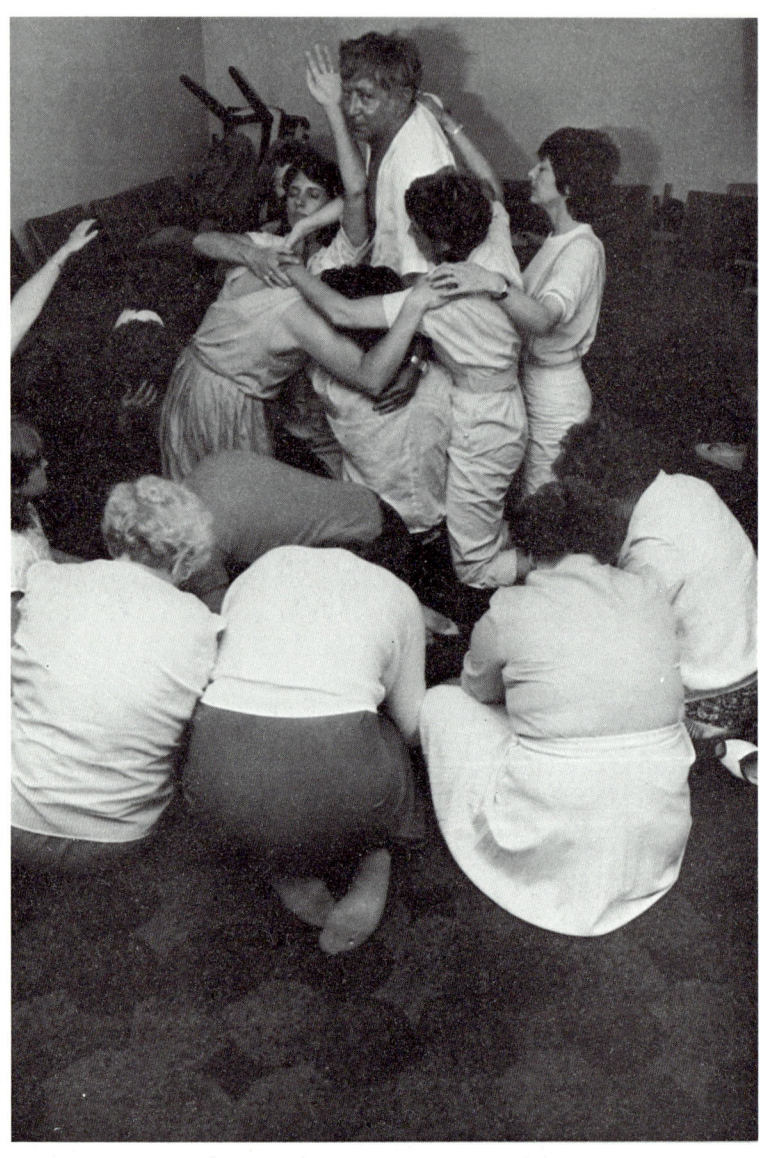

Kundalini, the bringing out of the 'Life Force' is demonstrated here; John Cain is strictly in control of the exercises of the Kundalini students.

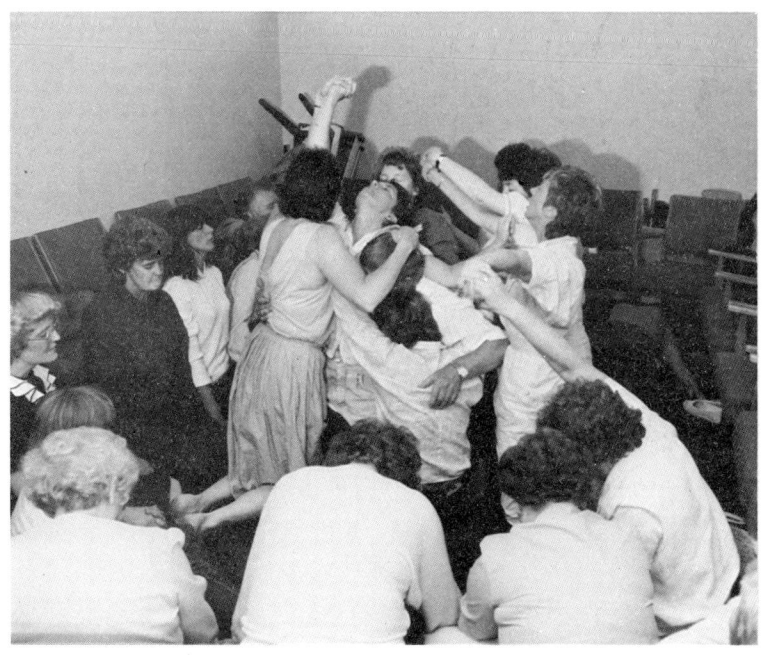

APPENDIX

[Three poems by Doreen Thomas]

THE knowledge we gain throughout our lives, formulates our personalities.

As rocks form over billions of years – so our ideals become entrenched.

How therefore do we set about the removal of old philosophies in order that we may delve deeper into our consciousness, and in so doing, allow finer ideals to formulate?

As the eruption of a volcano can rend assunder the immense density of rock in it's path, emitting colossal forces from it's depth – so, the sheer force of Kundalini can overcome the narrow outlooks and prejudices formulated over the centuries.

It will cast the bedrock of negativity assunder, and when the debris has subsided we will be left with a solid foundation on which to build a happier life. A life committed to love, peace and compassion. An endorsement to all, that the striving towards a state of higher consciousness can be achieved.

Our very survival depends upon the new life which will spring forth, it's roots held firm in the fertile soil of our enlightenment nurtured by our love and sustained by the force of Kundalini.

Surrender to the healing force
Reiterate to others
The Kundalini's vital source
A bridge to make men brothers.
With courage take the giant step
Be strong and firm and true
And prove to those who live in doubt
That if they try, they too
Can rise to higher planes of thought
Rejoicing in the knowledge
The path is clear and straight and true
There is no need to forage
Through an undergrowth of platitudes
For the message reacurring
Is, love your brother
Guide his hand
The power will be unerring.

Come with me into the light
Be humbled by it's touch
A witness to the heavenly might
Of love and peace and such
Eternal happiness
It's golden cloak spread wide
Inviting those with good intent
To cast all doubts aside.
Consolidate the knowledge held
Accept what you will gain
For knowledge is a precious gem
And nothing is in vain.
The truth that shines within the light
Will be a constant beacon
Reflect the light, discharge it's might
Your resolve, it must not weaken.
For only by such servitude
Can darkness be reverted
The disaster, prophesied for man,
In this way is averted.

Man's warring nature can't contrive
The harmony for which we strive.
Pollution of the air we breathe.
The habitat we can't retrieve.
His thoughts of evil and corruption
Will lead man to his own destruction.

It is the vital element
Of Kundalini that is sent
To dissipate the warring factions,
It's power and strength
Will quell the actions
Of men, who with such evil intent
The universe, assunder would rent.

If all mankind were conscious of
The Kundalini's power and love.
The knowledge held would turn the tide,
Salvation's door would open wide.
Adhering to the higher self
We, in our turn will gain a wealth
Of understanding for man's plight.
An element, that with foresight
Can rectify the human ill
Extinguish the ego – encourage the will
Of man to seek the path of peace
And by so doing,
The anguish will cease.

JOHN CAIN HEALING CENTRE